First Published in the UK in 2015 by Focus Education (UK) Ltd

Focus Education (UK) Ltd
Talking Point Conference and Exhibition Centre
Huddersfield Road
Scouthead
Saddleworth
OL4 4AG

Focus Education (UK) Ltd Reg. No 4507968

ISBN 978-1-909038-43-1

Companies, institutions and other organisations wishing to make bulk purchases of books published by Focus Education should contact their local bookstore or Focus Education direct:

Customer Services, Focus Education, Talking Point Conference and Exhibition Centre,
Huddersfield Road, Scouthead, Saddleworth, OL4 4AG
Tel 01457 821818 Fax 01457 878205

www.focus-education.co.uk
customerservice@focus-education.co.uk
Printed in Great Britain by Focus Education UK Ltd, Scouthead

Users should be fully aware that Ofsted may change any element of their descriptors and guidance. This document was wholly accurate at the date of publication.

focuseducationuk

focuseducation1

focus-education-uk-ltd

About the author

Ros Ferrara is a full-time consultant with Focus Education. Much of her recent work has been on developing all aspects of English, including the 2014 curriculum, able pupils in English and embedding grammar to improve writing.

Prior to joining Focus, Ros worked in a consultancy and advisory role for Lambeth LA. During this period, she led development work on the National Strategies highly successful EAL Programme, was the Literacy lead for the authority and Primary Strategy Manager. Ros led and managed a range of initiatives, including Every Child a Reader, Every Child a Writer and action research aimed at improving writing. Her role also involved working very closely with senior leaders in schools on developing leadership, improving the quality of teaching and other school improvement issues.

She is also an accredited additional inspector with Tribal and continues to undertake inspections.

Recent feedback:

Very professional: we had confidence in her judgements.

Style was relaxed and approachable. Good balance between listening and practical activities.

Ros was wonderful. The material was relevant and interesting. Ros's presentation skills were excellent. Her interactions with teachers were professional but relaxed.

Ros has transformed writing in the school.

The support received both by senior leaders, middle managers and classroom practitioners has been key to our becoming an outstanding school.

The consultancy Ros has given to my school has empowered my staff and the impact is already notable when I look at pupil outcomes.

Leading English
in your school

Contents

Being the subject leader

This section outlines some of the key elements of being the subject leader in your school.

Subject leader role

Key purpose: Accelerate progress and raise standards through securing high quality teaching, a rich curriculum and effective use of resources.

The diagram opposite outlines
the aspects of the subject leader role.

The following pages unpick each
of these elements in more detail
as a basis for self-evaluation.

Note: the ordering of these
elements does not imply any
prioritisation.

Subject leader role

Aspect 1	Vision and policy
Headline	This is about ensuring that there is a clear sense of direction and supporting guidance to ensure a systematic approach to teaching and assessment.
Self-evaluation questions	❑ Do we have a vision for the teaching of English in our school? Was it developed in partnership with staff? Is it widely understood? ❑ Can we articulate how we want children to develop as speakers, readers and writers? (i.e. what are the outcomes for learners?) ❑ Do we have a clear and simple English policy which helps staff understand the big picture for teaching English? ❑ Has our policy been reviewed to ensure that it is translated into practice?

Subject leader role

Aspect 2	Professional development
Headline	This is about ensuring that all staff are well equipped and skilled to teach English in an accurate and engaging way.
Self-evaluation questions	❑ Do we know the strengths and weaknesses of staff in terms of English subject knowledge and pedagogical knowledge? ❑ Do we have a professional development plan which addresses individual staff weakness? ❑ Is our professional development differentiated according to staff need? ❑ Does professional development model the way we want English taught? ❑ Do we check on the impact of our professional development spending? ❑ Do staff take responsibility for their own learning and development? ❑ Do staff know where to go for support? ❑ Is the subject leader seen as an approachable source of advice and guidance?

Subject leader role

Aspect 3	Monitoring and evaluation
Headline	This is about knowing about the quality of English in your school. Monitoring involves finding out and evaluating involves questioning whether things can be improved. The outcome of evaluation should be a simple self-evaluation summary which evidences what is working well and what needs to be improved.
Self-evaluation questions	❑ Have we got simple and effective systems for finding out what is happening with English teaching in the classroom? Does this involve using a range of methods to reach conclusions? ❑ Do we involve pupils in gathering feedback? ❑ Do we use work analysis as a valuable source of evidence? ❑ Do we routinely analyse assessment data both in a summative way and also formatively to identify next steps in teaching and learning? ❑ Can we confidently articulate how well children are making progress and how high standards are in English? ❑ Can we clearly identify what needs to be addressed to further improve English learning and progress for our pupils? ❑ Do we have a simple and succinct self-evaluation summary which states the position of English teaching within our school?

Subject leader role

Aspect 4	Improvement planning
Headline	Having identified the next steps for improvement in English, this is about putting a simple plan in place to bring about the improvement.

Self-evaluation questions	❏ Do we have a clear and simple improvement plan for English?
	❏ Does our plan include:
	   • Objectives
	   • Success criteria
	   • Actions
	   • Timescales
	   • Personnel
	   • Resources?
	   • How the actions will be monitored?
	❏ Is our plan evaluated with impact?
	❏ Is the plan understood by staff?
	❏ Is feedback provided to the leadership team and governors?

Subject leader role

Aspect 5	Curriculum
Headline	This is about ensuring that the English curriculum meets the requirements of the national curriculum and is delivered in a way that is engaging and relevant to children.

Self-evaluation questions	❑ Are we confident that the requirements of the national curriculum are met?
	❑ Can we evidence that English is being learnt in contexts which are both engaging and relevant for children?
	❑ Do we have a long term plan which evidences curricular coverage?
	❑ Do we have medium term plans which make clear what is being taught when, and is linked to the outcomes from assessment and needs of the class?
	❑ Do our medium term plans identify assessment opportunities?
	❑ Do we have clear short term plans in place which identify:
	    • Learning sequence
	    • Objectives and success criteria
	    • Vocabulary
	    • Teaching input - including differentiation and challenge
	    • Probing questions
	    • Deployment of other adults
	    • Assessment activities
	    • Cross curricular links

Subject leader role

Aspect 6	Assessment
Headline	This is about ensuring that appropriate and rigorous assessment is in place and that assessment information is used both summatively and formatively to impact on learning and progress.
Self-evaluation questions	❏ Do we have a clear understanding of the assessments we use in English? ❏ Do we have a clear understanding of when we use specific assessments in English? ❏ Are all staff skilled to use our assessments? ❏ Do staff have a range of strategies for assessing during the teaching sequence in order to steer teaching? ❏ Are we confident that assessment informs next steps in learning? ❏ Can we see clear evidence of peer and self assessment in English books? ❏ Can we see clear evidence of written feedback which impacts positively on next steps in English learning? ❏ Do teachers routinely use oral feedback to address misconceptions, exemplify teaching points and challenge children? ❏ Do staff routinely moderate work against agreed criteria to agree standards of work and next steps?

Subject leader role

Aspect 7	Learning environment and resources
Headline	This is about ensuring that English is well represented in the learning environment and ensuring that appropriate high quality resources are available and used to promote learning in English.
Self-evaluation questions	❑ Are there clear expectations about English in the learning environment? ❑ Does each teacher know what is expected in terms of English within their classroom environment? ❑ Is English represented on displays in the central area of the school? ❑ Does each classroom/learning space have appropriate resources and prompts which are readily available to children? ❑ Do staff know which resources are available for teaching each aspect of their English curriculum? ❑ Have you identified expertise within the staff and is this shared with other staff so that all know the 'go to' expert for specific areas?

Subject leader role

Aspect 8	Promotion of the subject
Headline	This is about ensuring that English has a high profile in the school.
Self-evaluation questions	❑ Do you ensure that English is included in the improvement plan? ❑ Do you keep staff up to date with developments in English? ❑ Do you include English learning in thematic teaching/theme weeks? ❑ Do you ensure that links are made between English and other areas of the curriculum? ❑ Do you regularly share aspects of English learning with parents and carers? ❑ Do you ensure that English learning for staff is fun, engaging and useful?

Getting the role in perspective

There are many people who still do not understand the central strand of subject leadership. All too often, the role is confined to tidying cupboards and labelling resources! Whilst this is important and has a place, it is important that subject leaders grasp the core purpose of the role and focus on answering a few key questions:

➢ How high are standards?
➢ How well are children progressing?
➢ Is this good enough?
➢ How effective is teaching, including assessment?
➢ Is it good enough?
➢ How well planned is the curriculum to raise standards and promote fundamental British values?
➢ Is it good enough?
➢ How effective is leadership and management?
➢ Is it good enough?

Underpinning each of these would be the sub-questions...

✧ How do you know?
✧ What next?

The diagram on the next page summarises the mind-set for subject leaders to focus these key questions.

Whatever your subject...

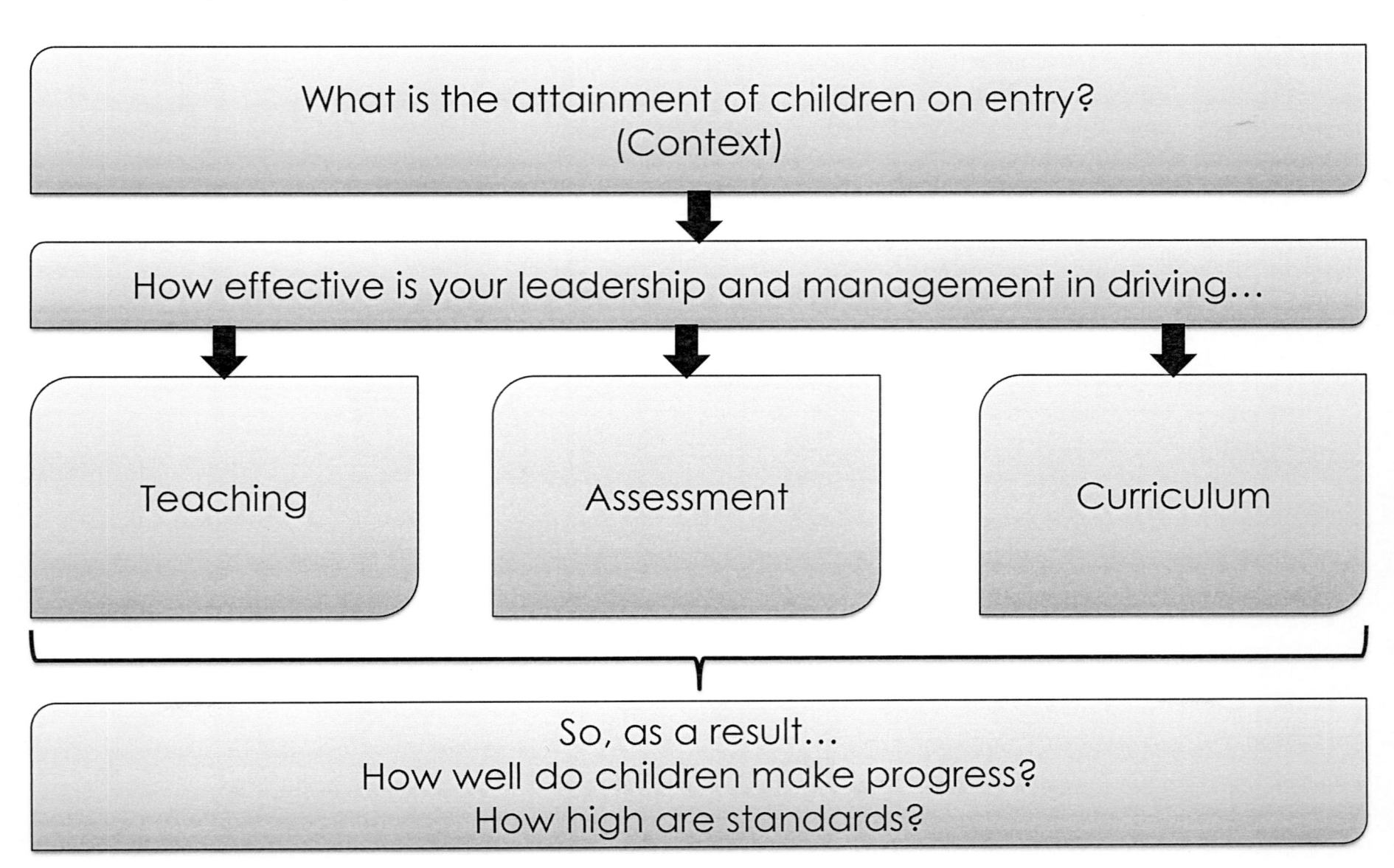

What is the attainment of children on entry?
(Context)

How effective is your leadership and management in driving...

Teaching

Assessment

Curriculum

So, as a result...
How well do children make progress?
How high are standards?

Questions for subject leaders

Questions for subject leaders

Many schools ask for a standard list of questions which subject leaders could consider, especially prior to an inspection. There is no standard list of questions to be used on inspection as it wholly depends on the school's own self evaluation, data and identified issues. If subject leaders consider the following model, they will be able to answer questions in all areas.

How effective is ... ?

How do you know?

What impact has your work had?

What are the next steps?

The specific questions on the following pages may also help subject leaders to think through issues.

Standards, Progress & Achievement

- What proportion of pupils meet age related expectations?
- How has this changed as the cohort has moved through the school?
- How well do pupils achieve in this subject?
- Is there any difference based on analysis of groups? (e.g. SEN, more able, pupil premium etc.)
- How well do disadvantaged pupils and/or vulnerable pupils achieve?
- How do you evaluate standards?
- Based on your evaluation, what are your improvement points?
- What have you done which has had a positive impact on outcomes? How do you know?
- Which aspect of the subject do the pupils achieve best in?

Assessment

- How effective are your assessment arrangements? How accurate are assessments?
- How do you moderate assessments?
- How is assessment used? What impact does this have?
- How do you track progress? Is this consistent?
- What does your tracking tell you?

Teaching & Learning

- [ ] How effective is teaching & learning in the subject?
- [ ] Which are the strongest/weakest elements?
- [ ] What most needs improving? What are you doing to address this?

Curriculum

- [ ] Which aspects of the subject are the strongest?
- [ ] Which aspects most need improving? What are you doing to address this?
- [ ] How do you ensure that basic skills are applied across the curriculum?
- [ ] How does your subject impact on learning in other subjects?
- [ ] How is enrichment used to impact on learning?
- [ ] How does this subject promote fundamental British values?
- [ ] How does this subject promote and support spiritual, moral, social and cultural development?

Leadership

- [ ] How effective is your leadership? How can you evidence this?
- [ ] What has been the impact of your leadership?
- [ ] How do you communicate new issues & expectations to colleagues?
- [ ] What has improved most in the past year? Two years?

Monitoring and Evaluation

- [ ] How do you monitor and evaluate?
- [ ] What has your evaluation led to? What has been the impact?
- [ ] How do you make sure you are getting a true picture of what is happening?

Statutory
Curriculum Coverage

This section outlines the English curriculum
as outlined in the National Curriculum 2014.

Spoken Language

**What the National Curriculum
requires in spoken language at KS1 and KS2**

Department for Education

Pupils should be taught to:

- Listen and respond appropriately to adults and their peers

- Ask relevant questions to extend their understanding and knowledge

- Use relevant strategies to build their vocabulary

- Articulate and justify answers, arguments and opinions

- Give well-structured descriptions, explanations and narratives for different purposes, including for expressing feelings

- Maintain attention and participate actively in collaborative conversations, staying on topic and initiating and responding to comments

- Use spoken language to develop understanding through speculating, hypothesising, imagining and exploring ideas

- Speak audibly and fluently with an increasing command of Standard English

- Participate in discussions, presentations, performances, role play, improvisations and debates

- Gain, maintain and monitor the interest of the listener(s)

- Consider and evaluate different viewpoints, attending to and building on the contributions of others

- Select and use appropriate registers for effective communication.

Reading

What the National Curriculum requires in reading at Y1

Word reading
- apply phonic knowledge and skills as the route to decode words
- respond speedily with the correct sound to graphemes (letters or groups of letters) for all 40+ phonemes, including, where applicable, alternative sounds for graphemes
- read accurately by blending sounds in unfamiliar words containing GPCs that have been taught
- read common exception words, noting unusual correspondences between spelling and sound and where these occur in the word
- read words containing taught GPCs and –s, –es, –ing, –ed, –er and –est endings
- read other words of more than one syllable that contain taught GPCs
- read words with contractions [for example, I'm, I'll, we'll], and understand that the apostrophe represents the omitted letter(s)
- read aloud accurately books that are consistent with their developing phonic knowledge and that do not require them to use other strategies to work out words
- re-read these books to build up their fluency and confidence in word reading.

Comprehension
- develop pleasure in reading, motivation to read, vocabulary and understanding by:
    - listening to and discussing a wide range of poems, stories and non-fiction at a level beyond that at which they can read independently
    - being encouraged to link what they read or hear read to their own experiences
    - becoming very familiar with key stories, fairy stories and traditional tales, retelling them and considering their particular characteristics
    - recognising and joining in with predictable phrases
    - learning to appreciate rhymes and poems, and to recite some by heart
    - discussing word meanings, linking new meanings to those already known
- understand both the books they can already read accurately and fluently and those they listen to by:
    - drawing on what they already know or on background information and vocabulary provided by the teacher
    - checking that the text makes sense to them as they read and correcting inaccurate reading
    - discussing the significance of the title and events
    - making inferences on the basis of what is being said and done
    - predicting what might happen on the basis of what has been read so far
- participate in discussion about what is read to them, taking turns and listening to what others say
- explain clearly their understanding of what is read to them.

What the National Curriculum requires in reading at Y2

Word reading

- continue to apply phonic knowledge and skills as the route to decode words until automatic decoding has become embedded and reading is fluent
- read accurately by blending the sounds in words that contain the graphemes taught so far, especially recognising alternative sounds for graphemes
- read accurately words of two or more syllables that contain the same graphemes as above
- read words containing common suffixes
- read further common exception words, noting unusual correspondences between spelling and sound and where these occur in the word
- read most words quickly and accurately, without overt sounding and blending, when they have been frequently encountered
- read aloud books closely matched to their improving phonic knowledge, sounding out unfamiliar words accurately, automatically and without undue hesitation
- re-read these books to build up their fluency and confidence in word reading.

Comprehension

- develop pleasure in reading, motivation to read, vocabulary and understanding by:
  - o listening to, discussing and expressing views about a wide range of contemporary and classic poetry, stories and non-fiction at a level beyond that at which they can read independently
  - o discussing the sequence of events in books and how items of information are related
  - o becoming increasingly familiar with and retelling a wider range of stories, fairy stories and traditional tales
  - o being introduced to non-fiction books that are structured in different ways
  - o recognising simple recurring literary language in stories and poetry
  - o discussing and clarifying the meanings of words, linking new meanings to known vocabulary
  - o discussing their favourite words and phrases
  - o continuing to build up a repertoire of poems learnt by heart, appreciating these and reciting some, with appropriate intonation to make the meaning clear
- understand both the books that they can already read accurately and fluently and those that they listen to by:
  - o drawing on what they already know or on background information and vocabulary provided by the teacher
  - o checking that the text makes sense to them as they read and correcting inaccurate reading
  - o making inferences on the basis of what is being said and done
  - o answering and asking questions
  - o predicting what might happen on the basis of what has been read so far
- participate in discussion about books, poems and other works that are read to them and those that they can read for themselves, taking turns and listening to what others say
- explain and discuss their understanding of books, poems and other material, both those that they listen to and those that they read for themselves.

What the National Curriculum requires in reading at Y3 and Y4

 Department for Education

Word reading

- apply their growing knowledge of root words, prefixes and suffixes (etymology and morphology) as listed in Appendix 1 of the National Curriculum, both to read aloud and to understand the meaning of new words they meet
- read further exception words, noting the unusual correspondences between spelling and sound, and where these occur in the word.

Comprehension

- develop positive attitudes to reading and understanding of what they read by:
    - listening to and discussing a wide range of fiction, poetry, plays, non-fiction and reference books or textbooks
    - reading books that are structured in different ways and reading for a range of purposes
    - using dictionaries to check the meaning of words that they have read
    - increasing their familiarity with a wide range of books, including fairy stories, myths and legends, and retelling some of these orally
    - identifying themes and conventions in a wide range of books
    - preparing poems and play scripts to read aloud and to perform, showing understanding through intonation, tone, volume and action
    - discussing words and phrases that capture the reader's interest and imagination
    - recognising some different forms of poetry [for example, free verse, narrative poetry]
- understand what they read, in books they can read independently, by:
    - checking that the text makes sense to them, discussing their understanding and explaining the meaning of words in context
    - asking questions to improve their understanding of a text
    - drawing inferences such as inferring characters' feelings, thoughts and motives from their actions, and justifying inferences with evidence
    - predicting what might happen from details stated and implied
    - identifying main ideas drawn from more than one paragraph and summarising these
    - identifying how language, structure, and presentation contribute to meaning
- retrieve and record information from non-fiction
- participate in discussion about both books that are read to them and those they can read for themselves, taking turns and listening to what others say.

What the National Curriculum requires in reading at Y5 and Y6

Word reading
- apply their growing knowledge of root words, prefixes and suffixes (morphology and etymology), as listed in Appendix 1 of the National Curriculum, both to read aloud and to understand the meaning of new words that they meet.

Comprehension
- maintain positive attitudes to reading and understanding of what they read by:
  o continuing to read and discuss an increasingly wide range of fiction, poetry, plays, non-fiction and reference books or textbooks
  o reading books that are structured in different ways and reading for a range of purposes
  o increasing their familiarity with a wide range of books, including myths, legends and traditional stories, modern fiction, fiction from our literary heritage, and books from other cultures and traditions
  o recommending books that they have read to their peers, giving reasons for their choices
  o identifying and discussing themes and conventions in and across a wide range of writing
  o making comparisons within and across books
  o learning a wider range of poetry by heart
  o preparing poems and plays to read aloud and to perform, showing understanding through intonation, tone and volume so that the meaning is clear to an audience
- understand what they read by:
  o checking that the book makes sense to them, discussing their understanding and exploring the meaning of words in context
  o asking questions to improve their understanding
  o drawing inferences such as inferring characters' feelings, thoughts and motives from their actions, and justifying inferences with evidence
  o predicting what might happen from details stated and implied
  o summarising the main ideas drawn from more than one paragraph, identifying key details that support the main ideas
  o identifying how language, structure and presentation contribute to meaning
- discuss and evaluate how authors use language, including figurative language, considering the impact on the reader
- distinguish between statements of fact and opinion
- retrieve, record and present information from non-fiction
- participate in discussions about books that are read to them and those they can read for themselves, building on their own and others' ideas and challenging views courteously
- explain and discuss their understanding of what they have read, including through formal presentations and debates, maintaining a focus on the topic and using notes where necessary
- provide reasoned justifications for their views.

Writing

Department for Education

What the National Curriculum requires in writing at Y1

Writing - transcription
- spell:
    - words containing each of the 40+ phonemes already taught
    - common exception words
    - the days of the week
- name the letters of the alphabet:
    - naming the letters of the alphabet in order
    - using letter names to distinguish between alternative spellings of the same sound
- add prefixes and suffixes:
    - using the spelling rule for adding –s or –es as the plural marker for nouns and the third person singular marker for verbs
    - using the prefix un–
    - using –ing, –ed, –er and –est where no change is needed in the spelling of root words [for example, helping, helped, helper, quicker, quickest]
- apply simple spelling rules and guidance, as listed in Appendix 1 of the National Curriculum
- write from memory simple sentences dictated by the teacher that include words using the GPCs and common exception words taught so far.

Handwriting
- sit correctly at a table, holding a pencil comfortably and correctly
- begin to form lower-case letters in the correct direction, starting and finishing in the right place
- form capital letters
- form digits 0-9
- understand which letters belong to which handwriting 'families' (i.e. letters that are formed in similar ways) and to practise these.

Writing - composition
- write sentences by:
    - saying out loud what they are going to write about
    - composing a sentence orally before writing it
    - sequencing sentences to form short narratives
    - re-reading what they have written to check that it makes sense
- discuss what they have written with the teacher or other pupils
- read aloud their writing clearly enough to be heard by their peers and the teacher.

- develop their understanding of the concepts set out in Appendix 2 of the National Curriculum by:
    - leaving spaces between words
    - joining words and joining clauses using and
    - beginning to punctuate sentences using a capital letter and a full stop, question mark or exclamation mark
    - using a capital letter for names of people, places, the days of the week, and the personal pronoun 'I'
    - learning the grammar for year 1 in English Appendix 2
- use the grammatical terminology in English Appendix 2 in discussing their writing.

What the National Curriculum requires in writing at Y2

Writing - transcription

- spell by:
  - segmenting spoken words into phonemes and representing these by graphemes, spelling many correctly
  - learning new ways of spelling phonemes for which one or more spellings are already known, and learn some words with each spelling, including a few common homophones
  - learning to spell common exception words
  - learning to spell more words with contracted forms
  - learning the possessive apostrophe (singular) [for example, the girl's book]
  - distinguishing between homophones and near-homophones
- add suffixes to spell longer words, including –ment, –ness, –ful, –less, –ly
- apply spelling rules and guidance, as listed in Appendix 1 of the National Curriculum
- write from memory simple sentences dictated by the teacher that include words using the GPCs, common exception words and punctuation taught so far.

Handwriting

- form lower-case letters of the correct size relative to one another
- start using some of the diagonal and horizontal strokes needed to join letters and understand which letters, when adjacent to one another, are best left unjoined
- write capital letters and digits of the correct size, orientation and relationship to one another and to lower case letters
- use spacing between words that reflects the size of the letters.

Writing - composition

- develop positive attitudes towards and stamina for writing by:
  - writing narratives about personal experiences and those of others (real and fictional)
  - writing about real events
  - writing poetry
  - writing for different purposes
- consider what they are going to write before beginning by:
  - planning or saying out loud what they are going to write about
  - writing down ideas and/or key words, including new vocabulary
  - encapsulating what they want to say, sentence by sentence
- make simple additions, revisions and corrections to their own writing by:
  - evaluating their writing with the teacher and other pupils
  - re-reading to check that their writing makes sense and that verbs to indicate time are used correctly and consistently, including verbs in the continuous form
  - proof-reading to check for errors in spelling, grammar and punctuation [for example, ends of sentences punctuated correctly]
- read aloud what they have written with appropriate intonation to make the meaning clear.

- develop their understanding of the concepts set out in Appendix 2 of the National Curriculum by:
  - learning how to use both familiar and new punctuation correctly (see English Appendix 2), including full stops, capital letters, exclamation marks, question marks, commas for lists and apostrophes for contracted forms and the possessive (singular)
- learn how to use:
  - sentences with different forms: statement, question, exclamation, command
  - expanded noun phrases to describe and specify [for example, the blue butterfly]
  - the present and past tenses correctly and consistently including the progressive form
  - subordination (using when, if, that, or because) and co-ordination (using or, and, or but)
  - the grammar for year 2 in English Appendix 2
  - some features of written Standard English
- use and understand the grammatical terminology in English

What the National Curriculum requires in writing at Y3 and Y4

Writing - transcription

- use further prefixes and suffixes and understand how to add them (English Appendix 1)
- spell further homophones
- spell words that are often misspelt (English Appendix 1)
- place the possessive apostrophe accurately in words with regular plurals [for example, girls', boys'] and in words with irregular plurals [for example, children's]
- use the first two or three letters of a word to check its spelling in a dictionary
- write from memory simple sentences, dictated by the teacher, that include words and punctuation taught so far.

Handwriting

- use the diagonal and horizontal strokes that are needed to join letters and understand which letters, when adjacent to one another, are best left unjoined
- increase the legibility, consistency and quality of their handwriting [for example, by ensuring that the downstrokes of letters are parallel and equidistant; that lines of writing are spaced sufficiently so that the ascenders and descenders of letters do not touch].

Writing - composition

- plan their writing by:
  - discussing writing similar to that which they are planning to write in order to understand and learn from its structure, vocabulary and grammar
  - discussing and recording ideas
- draft and write by:
  - composing and rehearsing sentences orally (including dialogue), progressively building a varied and rich vocabulary and an increasing range of sentence structures – see Appendix 2 of the National Curriculum
  - organising paragraphs around a theme
  - in narratives, creating settings, characters and plot
  - in non-narrative material, using simple organisational devices [for example, headings and sub-headings]
- evaluate and edit by:
  - assessing the effectiveness of their own and others' writing and suggesting improvements
  - proposing changes to grammar and vocabulary to improve consistency, including the accurate use of pronouns in sentences
- proof-read for spelling and punctuation errors
- read aloud their own writing, to a group or the whole class, using appropriate intonation and controlling the tone and volume so that the meaning is clear.

- develop their understanding of the concepts set out in Appendix 2 of the National Curriculum by:
  - extending the range of sentences with more than one clause by using a wider range of conjunctions, including when, if, because, although
  - using the present perfect form of verbs in contrast to the past tense
  - choosing nouns or pronouns appropriately for clarity and cohesion and to avoid repetition
  - using conjunctions, adverbs and prepositions to express time and cause
  - using fronted adverbials
  - learning the grammar for years 3 and 4 in English Appendix 2
- indicate grammatical and other features by:
  - using commas after fronted adverbials
  - indicating possession by using the possessive apostrophe with plural nouns
  - using and punctuating direct speech
- use and understand the grammatical terminology in English Appendix 2 accurately and appropriately when discussing their writing and reading.

What the National Curriculum requires in writing at Y5 and Y6

Writing - transcription
- use further prefixes and suffixes and understand the guidance for adding them
- spell some words with 'silent' letters [for example, knight, psalm, solemn]
- continue to distinguish between homophones and other words which are often confused
- use knowledge of morphology and etymology in spelling and understand that the spelling of some words needs to be learnt specifically, as listed in English Appendix 1
- use dictionaries to check the spelling and meaning of words
- use the first three or four letters of a word to check spelling, meaning or both of these in a dictionary
- use a thesaurus

Handwriting
- write legibly, fluently and with increasing speed by:
  - choosing which shape of a letter to use when given choices and deciding whether or not to join specific letters
  - choosing the writing implement that is best suited for a task.

Writing - composition
- plan their writing by:
  - identifying the audience for and purpose of the writing, selecting the appropriate form and using other similar writing as models for their own
  - noting and developing initial ideas, drawing on reading and research where necessary
  - in writing narratives, considering how authors have developed characters and settings in what pupils have read, listened to or seen performed
- draft and write by:
  - selecting appropriate grammar and vocabulary, understanding how such choices can change and enhance meaning
  - in narratives, describing settings, characters and atmosphere and integrating dialogue to convey character and advance the action
  - précising longer passages
  - using a wide range of devices to build cohesion within and across paragraphs
  - using further organisational and presentational devices to structure text and to guide the reader [for example, headings, bullet points, underlining]
- evaluate and edit by:
  - assessing the effectiveness of their own and others' writing
  - proposing changes to vocabulary, grammar and punctuation to enhance effects and clarify meaning
  - ensuring the consistent and correct use of tense throughout a piece of writing
  - ensuring correct subject and verb agreement when using singular and plural, distinguishing between the language of speech and writing and choosing the appropriate register
- proof-read for spelling and punctuation errors
- perform their own compositions, using appropriate intonation, volume, and movement so that meaning is clear.

- develop their understanding of the concepts set out in Appendix 2 of the National Curriculum by:
  - recognising vocabulary and structures that are appropriate for formal speech and writing, including subjunctive forms
  - using passive verbs to affect the presentation of information in a sentence
  - using the perfect form of verbs to mark relationships of time and cause
  - using expanded noun phrases to convey complicated information concisely
  - using modal verbs or adverbs to indicate degrees of possibility
  - using relative clauses beginning with who, which, where, when, whose, that or with an implied (i.e. omitted) relative pronoun
  - learning the grammar for years 5 and 6 in English Appendix 2
- indicate grammatical and other features by:
  - using commas to clarify meaning or avoid ambiguity in writing
  - using hyphens to avoid ambiguity
  - using brackets, dashes or commas to indicate parenthesis
  - using semi-colons, colons or dashes to mark boundaries between independent clauses
  - using a colon to introduce a list
  - punctuating bullet points consistently
- use and understand the grammatical terminology in English Appendix 2 accurately and appropriately in discussing their writing and reading.

Key Assessment Criteria

The key assessment criteria for English have been devised in such a way that they can be applied in all settings, regardless of the agreed programme of study. These criteria allow teachers to assess how well children are developing as speakers, readers and writers.

Teachers may wish to supplement these key assessment criteria with other criteria if they feel that this adds value.

Key Assessment Criteria: *Being a speaker*

A year 1 speaker	A year 2 speaker	A year 3 speaker
• I speak clearly and confidently in front of people in my class. • I can re-tell a well known story and remember the main characters. • I can hold attention when playing and learning with others. • I can keep to the main topic when we are talking in a group. • I can ask questions in order to get more information. • I can start a conversation with an adult I know well or with my friends. • I listen carefully to the things other people have to say in a group. • I join in with conversations in a group. • I join in with role play.	• I can ask questions to get more information and clarify meaning. • I can talk in complete sentences. • I can decide when I need to use specific vocabulary. • I can take turns when talking in pairs or a small group. • I am aware that formal and informal situations require different language (beginning). • I can retell a story using narrative language and linking words and phrases. • I can hold the attention of people I am speaking to by adapting the way I talk. • I understand how to speak for different purposes and audiences (beginning). • I can perform a simple poem from memory.	• I can sequence and communicate ideas in an organised and logical way, always using complete sentences. • I vary the amount of detail and choice of vocabulary, depending on the purpose and the audience. • I take a full part in paired and group discussions. • I show that I know when Standard English is required and use it (beginning). • I can retell a story using narrative language and add relevant detail. • I can show that I have listened carefully because I make relevant comments. • I can present ideas or information to an audience. • I recognise that meaning can be expressed in different ways, depending on the context. • I can perform poems from memory adapting expression and tone as appropriate.

Key Assessment Criteria: *Being a speaker*

A year 4 speaker	A year 5 speaker	A year 6 speaker
• I ask questions to clarify or develop my understanding.	• I can engage the listener by varying my expression and vocabulary.	• I talk confidently and fluently in a range of situations, using formal and Standard English, if necessary.
• I can sequence, develop and communicate ideas in an organised and logical way, always using complete sentences.	• I adapt my spoken language depending on the audience, the purpose or the context.	• I ask questions to develop ideas and take account of others' views.
• I show that I understand the main point and the details in a discussion.	• I can develop my ideas and opinions, providing relevant detail.	• I explain ideas and opinions giving reasons and evidence.
• I adapt what I am saying to the needs of the listener or audience (increasingly).	• I can express my point of view.	• I take an active part in discussions and can take on different roles.
• I show that I know that language choices vary in different contexts.	• I show that I understand the main points, including implied meanings in a discussion.	• I listen to, and consider the opinions of, others in discussions.
• I can present to an audience using appropriate intonation; controlling the tone and volume so that the meaning is clear.	• I listen carefully in discussions. I make contributions and ask questions that are responsive to others' ideas and views.	• I make contributions to discussions, evaluating others' ideas and respond to them.
• I can justify an answer by giving evidence.	• I use Standard English in formal situations.	• I can sustain and argue a point of view in a debate, using the formal language of persuasion.
• I use Standard English when it is required.	• I am beginning to use hypothetical language to consider more than one possible outcome or solution.	• I can express possibilities using hypothetical and speculative language.
• I cam perform poems or plays from memory, conveying ideas about characters and situations by adapting expression and tone.	• I can perform my own compositions, using appropriate intonation and volume so that meaning is clear.	• I engage listeners through choosing appropriate vocabulary and register that is matched to the context.
	• I can perform poems and plays from memory, making careful choices about how I convey ideas. I adapt my expression and tone.	• I can perform my own compositions, using appropriate intonation, volume and expression so that literal and implied meaning is clear.
	• I begin to select the appropriate register according to the context.	• I can perform poems and plays from memory, making deliberate choices about how to convey ideas about characters, contexts and atmosphere.

KS1 Reading 2016:
The expected standard

In preparing for the new statutory assessment arrangements in 2016, the government has identified the bullet points below as the 'expected standard' in reading by the end of Key Stage One.

Making inferences
- Make simple and general inferences based on the text
- Make simple and general predictions based on the text

Comprehension
- Identify the meaning of vocabulary in context
- Identify sequences of events in a range of straightforward texts
- Identify how information is related and/or organised within texts

Provide simple explanations for:
- The significance of titles in fiction and non-fiction texts
- Events and characters' actions
- Key information
- Retrieve details from fiction and non-fiction to demonstrate understanding of character, events and information

Language for effect
- Identify simple and recurring literary language

KS2 Reading 2016:
The expected standard

In preparing for the new statutory assessment arrangements in 2016, the government has identified the bullet points below as the 'expected standard' in reading by the end of Key Stage Two.

Themes and conventions
- Accurately identify the features, themes and conventions of a range of fiction
- Accurately identify the features, themes and conventions of a range of non-fiction text types and forms
- Draw on evidence within texts to explain how themes emerge and conventions are applied in a range of genres and conventions of fiction and non-fiction

Making inferences
- Make developed inferences drawing on evidence from the text
- Explain and justify inferences, providing evidence from the text to support reasoning
- Make developed predictions that are securely rooted in the text

Comprehension
- Show an understanding of the meaning of vocabulary in context
- Accurately and selectively summarise main ideas, events, characters and information in fiction and non-fiction texts
- Identify language, structural and presentational features used in texts
- Provide developed explanation for key information and events and characters' actions and motivations
- Provide straightforward explanations for the purpose of the language, structure and presentation of texts
- Retrieve key details and quotations from fiction and non-fiction to demonstrate understanding of character, events and information
- Make accurate and appropriate comparisons within texts
- Correctly distinguish between statements of fact and opinion

Language for effect
- Identify a range of figurative language
- Explain the effect of figurative language

Key Assessment Criteria: *Being a reader*

A year 1 reader

Word reading

- I can match all 40+ graphemes to their phonemes.

- I can blend sounds in unfamiliar words.

- I can divide words into syllables.

- I can read compound words.

- I can read words with contractions and understand that the apostrophe represents the missing letters.

- I can read phonetically decodable words.

- I can read words that end with 's, -ing, -ed, -est

- I can read words which start with un-.

- I can add –ing, -ed and –er to verbs. (Where no change is needed to the root word)

- I can read words of more than one syllable that contain taught GPCs.

Comprehension

- I can say what I like and do not like about a text.

- I can link what I have heard or read to my own experiences.

- I can retell key stories orally using narrative language.

- I can talk about the main characters within a well known story.

- I can learn some poems and rhymes by heart.

- I can use what I already know to understand texts.

- I can check that my reading makes sense and go back to correct when it doesn't.

- I can draw inferences from the text and/or the illustrations. (Beginning)

- I can make predictions about the events in the text.

- I can explain what I think a text is about.

Key Assessment Criteria: *Being a reader*

A year 2 reader

Word reading

- I can decode automatically and fluently.

- I can blend sounds in words that contain the graphemes we have learnt.

- I can recognise and read alternative sounds for graphemes.

- I can read accurately words of two or more syllables that contain the same GPCs.

- I can read words with common suffixes.

- I can read common exception words.

- I can read and comment on unusual correspondence between grapheme and phoneme.

- I read most words quickly and accurately when I have read them before without sounding out and blending.

- I can read most suitable books accurately, showing fluency and confidence.

Comprehension

- I can talk about and give an opinion on a range of texts.

- I can discuss the sequence of events in books and how they relate to each other.

- I use prior knowledge, including context and vocabulary, to understand texts.

- I can retell stories, including fairy stories and traditional tales.

- I can read for meaning and check that the text makes sense. I go back and re-read when it does not makes sense.

- I can find recurring language in stories and poems.

- I can talk about my favourite words and phrases in stories and poems.

- I can recite some poems by heart, with appropriate intonation.

- I can answer and ask questions.

- I can make predictions based on what I have read.

- I can draw (simple) inferences from illustrations, events, characters' actions and speech.

Key Assessment Criteria: *Being a reader*

A year 3 reader

Word reading

- I can apply knowledge of root words, prefixes and suffixes to read aloud and to understand the meaning of unfamiliar words.

- I can read further exception words, noting the unusual correspondences between spelling and sound.

- I attempt pronunciation of unfamiliar words drawing on prior knowledge of similar looking words.

Comprehension

- I read a range of fiction, poetry, plays, and non-fiction texts.

- I can discuss the texts that I read.

- I can read aloud and independently, taking turns and listening to others.

- I can explain how non-fiction books are structured in different ways and can use them effectively.

- I can explain some of the different types of fiction books.

- I can ask relevant questions to get a better understanding of a text.

- I can predict what might happen based on details I have.

- I can draw inferences such as inferring characters' feelings, thoughts and motives from their actions.

- I can use a dictionary to check the meaning of unfamiliar words.

- I can identify the main point of a text.

- I can explain how structure and presentation contribute to the meaning of texts.

- I can use non-fiction texts to retrieve information.

- I can prepare poems to read aloud and to perform, showing understanding through intonation, tone, volume and action.

Key Assessment Criteria: *Being a reader*

A year 4 reader

Word reading

- I can apply knowledge of root words, prefixes and suffixes to read aloud and to understand the meaning of unfamiliar words.

- I can read further exception words, noting the unusual correspondences between spelling and sound.

- I attempt pronunciation of unfamiliar words drawing on prior knowledge of similar looking words.

Comprehension

- I know which books to select for specific purposes, especially in relation to science, geography and history learning.

- I can use a dictionary to check the meaning of unfamiliar words.

- I can discuss and record words and phrases that writers use to engage and impact on the reader.

- I can identify some of the literary conventions in different texts.

- I can identify the (simple) themes in texts.

- I can prepare poems to read aloud and to perform, showing understanding through intonation, tone, volume and action.

- I can explain the meaning of words in context.

- I can ask relevant questions to improve my understanding of a text.

- I can infer meanings and begin to justify them with evidence from the text.

- I can predict what might happen from details stated and from the information I have deduced.

- I can identify where a writer has used precise word choices for effect to impact on the reader.

- I can identify some text type organisational features, for example, narrative, explanation and persuasion.

- I can retrieve information from non-fiction texts.

- I can build on others' ideas and opinions about a text in discussion.

Key Assessment Criteria: *Being a reader*

A year 5 reader

Word reading

- I can apply knowledge of root words, prefixes and suffixes to read aloud and to understand the meaning of unfamiliar words.

- I can read further exception words, noting the unusual correspondences between spelling and sound.

- I attempt pronunciation of unfamiliar words drawing on prior knowledge of similar looking words.

- I can re-read and read ahead to check for meaning.

Comprehension

- I am familiar with and can talk about a wide range of books and text types, including myths, legends and traditional stories and books from other cultures and traditions. I can discuss the features of each.

- I can read non-fiction texts and identify the purpose, structure and grammatical features, evaluating how effective they are.

- I can identify significant ideas, events and characters; and discuss their significance.

- I can recite poems by heart, e.g. narrative verse, haiku.

- I can prepare poems and plays to read aloud and to perform, showing understanding through intonation, tone, volume and action.

Key Assessment Criteria: *Being a reader*

A year 6 reader

Word reading

- I can apply knowledge of root words, prefixes and suffixes to read aloud and to understand the meaning of unfamiliar words.

- I use my combined knowledge of phonemes and word deriviations to pronounce words correctly, e.g. ara<u>ch</u>no<u>ph</u>obia.

- I attempt the pronunciation of unfamiliar words drawing on my prior knowledge of similar looking words.

- I can read fluently, using punctuation to inform meaning.

Comprehension

- I am familiar with and can talk about a wide range of books and text types, including myths, legends and traditional stories and books from other cultures and traditions. I can discuss the features of each.

- I can read books that are structured in different ways.

- I can recognise texts that contain features from more than one text type.

- I can evaluate how effectively texts are structured and presented.

- I can read non-fiction texts to help with my learning.

- I read accurately and check that I understand.

- I can recommend books to others and give reasons for my recommendation.

- I can identify themes in texts.

- I can identify and discuss the conventions in different text types.

- I can identify the key points in a text.

- I can recite a range of poems by heart, e.g. narrative verse, sonnet.

- I can prepare poems and plays to read aloud and to perform, showing understanding through intonation, tone, volume and action.

KS1 Grammar, punctuation & spelling 2016: The expected standard

2016

In preparing for the new statutory assessment arrangements in 2016, the government has identified the bullet points below as the 'expected standard' in grammar, punctuation and spelling by the end of Key Stage One.

Punctuation
- Identify and use appropriate end punctuation for demarcating different sentence types (full stop, question mark and exclamation mark)
- Identify and use a capital letter to start a sentence, for names and for the personal pronoun I
- Identify and insert commas in a list of single words
- Use apostrophes to construct simple contracted verb forms from given full forms, using correct spelling
- Identify the correct use of the apostrophe to denote singular possession and sometimes use the apostrophe correctly for this purpose.

Spelling
- Usually accurately spell simple monosyllabic and polysyllabic words, including high-frequency homophones and near-homophones in context
- Draw on their developing phonological, morphological and lexical awareness to apply the rules and patterns set out in the statutory Appendix 1 of the 2014 national curriculum.

KS1 Grammar, punctuation & spelling 2016: The expected standard

2016

In preparing for the new statutory assessment arrangements in 2016, the government has identified the bullet points below as the 'expected standard' in grammar, punctuation and spelling by the end of Key Stage One.

- Use some variety of sentence types as is appropriate to the given task, e.g. commands to instruct the reader; statements to give information.
- Able to introduce additional detail in their writing through the use of, for example, adjectives (including comparatives), adverbs, or simple expanded noun phrases (e.g. *the small cottage / the small cottage with the red door*).
- Clauses are mostly joined with co-ordinating conjunctions (*and, but, or*), with some use of subordination (e.g. to indicate cause or time).
- Tense is appropriate and mostly consistent in simple and progressive past and present forms.
- Sentences are usually demarcated with capital letters and full stops, or with appropriate use of question and exclamation marks.
- Capital letters are used to mark some proper nouns and always for the personal pronoun 'I'. There is some use of internal sentence punctuation, including commas to separate items in a list and apostrophes to mark contracted forms.
- Handwriting is legible. Capital and lower-case letters are accurately and consistently formed with appropriate spacing and consistent size.

KS1 Grammar, punctuation & spelling 2016: The expected standard

2016

In preparing for the new statutory assessment arrangements in 2016, the government has identified the bullet points below as the 'expected standard' in grammar, punctuation and spelling by the end of Key Stage One.

Grammar and vocabulary

- Demonstrate familiarity with some word classes and their use, including nouns, verbs, adjectives and adverbs
- Apply this terminology to identify familiar words within each word class when presented in a context
- Recognise different types of sentences, including statements, questions, commands and exclamations
- Write different types of sentences including statements, questions, commands and exclamations when prompted
- Understand that the coordinating conjunctions *and*, *or*, *but* link words and clauses and use them to construct and extend sentences
- Add a subordinate clause to a main clause using a simple subordinating conjunction (e.g. *when, if, because, that*) when prompted
- Combine or expand given words to make noun phrases, clauses or sentences
- Identify the present or past tense forms of familiar, regular verbs and some high-frequency irregular verbs (e.g. *has / had*)
- Apply correct endings to regular verb forms to indicate present and past tense, including the progressive form to mark actions in progress (e.g. *the lion is running / Ellie was shouting*)
- Demonstrate Standard English subject-verb agreement (e.g. *we were* as opposed to *we was*)
- Identify and select some appropriate language for the context such as formal, informal or Standard English as appropriate
- Understand that the prefix *un-* can change the meaning of some words
- Use some straightforward suffixes to form nouns and adjectives, including the suffixes *–er* and *–est* to form comparative adjectives.

KS2 Grammar, punctuation & spelling 2016: The expected standard

2016

In preparing for the new statutory assessment arrangements in 2016, the government has identified the bullet points below as the 'expected standard' in grammar, punctuation and spelling by the end of Key Stage Two.

Grammar

- Demonstrate familiarity with a range of word classes and their use, including nouns, verbs, adjectives, conjunctions, pronouns, adverbs, prepositions and determiners;
- Apply this terminology to identify familiar words within each word class when presented in a context;
- Recognise and write different types of sentences, including statements, questions, commands and exclamations;
- Demonstrate familiarity with terms relating to a sentence, including subject and object;
- Distinguish between co-ordinating and subordinating conjunctions and use them to link clauses appropriately;
- Identify and use main clauses and subordinate clauses (including relative clauses) in a sentence and construct expanded noun phrases for description and concision;
- Identify and construct fronted adverbial phrases to denote time and place (e.g.: *Later that day, I met Tina.*);
- Select pronouns appropriately for clarity and cohesion (e.g. **The children** will be visiting the **activity centre. They** will try all the activities **it** has to offer.);
- Distinguish between formal and informal varieties of English (e.g. active / passive, subjunctive) and Standard and non-Standard varieties of English (e.g. use of *I* and *me*);
- Use Standard English and formal or informal structures when appropriate;
- Select and construct regular and irregular verb forms that express present and past time, including the progressive and perfect forms (e.g. *We are hoping to win. I had swum across the lake.*);
- Choose tenses accurately and mostly consistently;
- Ensure that subject and verb agree when using singular and plural nouns in a sentence;
- Identify the active and passive voice in terms of sentence structure; identify modal verbs to express future time and possibility (e.g. *I might go to the park. They should be home soon.*);
- Identify, form and expand contractions accurately;
- Select appropriate synonyms and antonyms for a wide range of words;
- Use prefixes and suffixes to change the meaning of words, for example, to change words into different word classes;
- Recognise and use words from the same word families.

KS2 Grammar, punctuation & spelling 2016: The expected standard

2016

In preparing for the new statutory assessment arrangements in 2016, the government has identified the bullet points below as the 'expected standard' in grammar, punctuation and spelling by the end of Key Stage Two.

Punctuation
- Demarcate sentences accurately, using capital letters and full stops, question marks or exclamation marks as appropriate;
- Use commas to mark clauses or phrases, including fronted adverbials, (eg: *The cottage, which had a blue door, looked warm and cosy. Despite these facts, people choose to eat unhealthy food*.) but they may not be able to use them consistently;
- Use inverted commas to denote speech and place these correctly in relation to internal punctuation;
- Use apostrophes correctly for omission and singular possession, and mostly accurately for plural possession;
- Identify where punctuation is used to indicate parenthesis;
- Identify colons, semi-colons, single dashes and hyphens but may not be able to use them consistently.

Spelling
- Spell accurately in general, including polysyllabic words that conform to regular patterns and some common exceptions to these, and less common prefixes and suffixes, for example *ir-*, *il-*, *-cian*, *-ous*;
- Spell or select the correct forms of common homophones; and
- Draw on their phonological, morphological and lexical awareness to apply the common rules and patterns and spell correctly a wide range of words, including those set out in statutory Appendix 1 of the 2014 national curriculum.

Key Assessment Criteria: *Being a writer*

A year 1 writer

Transcription

Spelling

- I can identify known phonemes in unfamiliar words.

- I can use syllables to divide words when spelling.

- I use what I know about alternative phonemes to narrow down possibilities for accurate spelling.

- I can use the spelling rule for adding 's' or 'es' for verbs in the 3rd person singular.

- I can name all the letters of the alphabet in order.

- I can use letter names to show alternative spellings of the same phoneme.

Handwriting

- I can sit correctly at a table, holding a pencil comfortable and correctly.

- I can form lower case letters in the correct direction, starting and finishing in the right place.

- I can form capital letters and digits 0-9.

Composition

- I can compose a sentence orally before writing it.

- I can sequence sentences in chronological order to recount and event or experience.

- I can re-read what I have written to check that it makes sense.

- I leave spaces between words.

- I know how the prefix 'un' can be added to words to change meaning.

- I can use the suffixes 's', 'es', 'ed', and 'ing' within my writing.

Grammar and punctuation

Sentence structure

- I can combine words to make a sentence.

- I can join two sentences using 'and'.

Text structure

- I can sequence sentences to form a narrative.

Punctuation

- I can separate words using finger spaces.

- I can use capital letters to start a sentence.

- I can use a full stop to end a sentence.

- I can use a question mark.

- I can use an exclamation mark.

- I can use capital letters for names.

- I can use 'I'.

Key Assessment Criteria: *Being a writer*

A year 2 writer

Transcription

Spelling

- I can segment spoken words into phonemes and record these as graphemes.

- I can spell words with alternatives spellings, including a few common homophones.

- I can spell longer words using suffixes such as 'ment', 'ness', 'ful', 'less', 'ly'.

- I can use my knowledge of alternative phonemes to narrow down possibilities for accurate spelling.

- I can identify phonemes in unfamiliar words and use syllables to divide words.

Handwriting

- I can form lower-case letters of the correct size relative to one another.

- I can begin to use some of the diagonal and horizontal strokes needed to join letters.

- I show that I know which letters are best left unjoined.

- I use capital letters and digits of the correct size, orientation and relationship to one another and to lower case letters.

- I use spacing between words that reflects the size of the letters.

Composition

- I can write narratives about personal experiences and those of others, both real and fictional.

- I can write for different purposes, including real events.

- I can plan and discuss the content of writing and record my ideas.

- I am able to orally rehearse structured sentences or sequences of sentences.

- I can evaluate my own writing independently, with friends and with an adult.

- I can proof-read to check for errors in spelling, grammar and punctuation.

Grammar and punctuation

Sentence structure

- I can use subordination and co-ordination.

- I can use expanded noun phrases.

- I can say how the grammatical patterns in a sentence indicate its function.

Text structure

- I consistently use the present tense and past tense correctly.

- I can use the progressive forms of verbs in the present and past tense.

Punctuation

- I use capital letters for names of people, places, day of the week and the personal pronoun 'I'.

- I correctly use question marks and exclamation marks,

- I can use commas to separate items in a list.

- I can use apostrophes to show where letters are missing and to mark singular possession in nouns.

Key Assessment Criteria: *Being a writer*

A year 3 writer

Transcription

Spelling

- I can spell words with additional prefixes and suffixes and understand how to add them to root words.

- I recognise and spell homophones.

- I can use the first two or three letters of a word to check its spelling in a dictionary.

- I can spell words correctly which are in a family.

- I can spell the commonly mis-spelt words from the Y3/4 word list.

- I can identify the root in longer words.

Handwriting

- I use the diagonal and horizontal strokes that are needed to join letters.

- I understand which letters should be left unjoined.

Composition

- I can discuss models of writing, noting its structure, grammatical features and use of vocabulary.

- I can compose sentences using a wider range of structures.

- I can write a narrative with a clear structure, setting, characters and plot.

- I can write non-narrative using simple organisational devices such as headings and sub-headings.

- I can suggest improvements to my own writing and that of others.

- I can make improvements to grammar, vocabulary and punctuation.

- I use a range of sentences with more than one clause by using a range of conjunctions.

- I use the perfect form of verbs to mark the relationship of time and cause.

- I can proof-read to check for errors in spelling and punctuation.

Grammar and punctuation

Sentence structure

- I can express time, place and cause by using conjunctions, adverbs and prepositions.

Text structure

- I am starting to use paragraphs.

- I can use headings and sub headings.

- I can use the present perfect form of verbs instead of the simple past.

Punctuation

- I can use inverted commas to punctuate direct speech.

Key Assessment Criteria: *Being a writer*

A year 4 writer

Transcription

Spelling

- I can spell words with prefixes and suffixes and can add them to root words.

- I can recognise and spell homophones.

- I can use the first two or three letters of a word to check a spelling in a dictionary.

- I can spell the commonly mis-spelt words from the Y3/4 word list.

Handwriting

- I can use the diagonal and horizontal strokes that are needed to join letters.

- I understand which letters should be left unjoined.

- My handwriting is legible and consistent; down strokes of letters are parallel and equidistant; lines of writing are spaced sufficiently so that ascenders and descenders of letters do not touch.

Composition

- I can compose sentences using a range of sentence structures.

- I can orally rehearse a sentence or a sequence of sentences.

- I can write a narrative with a clear structure, setting and plot.

- I can improve my writing by changing grammar and vocabulary to improve consistency.

- I use a range of sentences which have more than one clause.

- I can use appropriate nouns and pronouns within and across sentences to support cohesion and avoid repetition.

- I can use direct speech in my writing and punctuate it correctly.

Grammar and punctuation

Sentence structure

- I can use noun phrases which are expanded by adding modifying adjectives, nouns and preposition phrases.

- I can use fronted adverbials.

Text structure

- I can write in paragraphs.

- I make an appropriate choice of pronoun and noun within and across sentences.

Punctuation

- I can use inverted commas and other punctuation to indicate direct speech.

- I can use apostrophes to mark plural possession.

- I use commas after fronted adverbials.

Key Assessment Criteria: *Being a writer*

A year 5 writer

Transcription

Spelling

- I can form verbs with prefixes.

- I can convert nouns or adjectives into verbs by adding a suffix.

- I understand the rules for adding prefixes and suffixes.

- I can spell words with silent letters.

- I can distinguish between homophones and other words which are often confused.

- I can spell the commonly mis-spelt words from the Y5/6 word list.

- I can use the first 3 or 4 letters of a word to check spelling, meaning or both in a dictionary.

- I can use a thesaurus.

- I can use a range of spelling strategies.

Handwriting

- I can choose the style of handwriting to use when given a choice.

- I can choose the handwriting that is best suited for a specific task.

Composition

- I can discuss the audience and purpose of the writing.

- I can start sentences in different ways.

- I can use the correct features and sentence structure matched to the text type we are working on.

- I can develop characters through action and dialogue.

- I can establish a viewpoint as the writer through commenting on characters and events.

- I can use grammar and vocabulary to create an impact on the reader.

- I can use stylistic devices to create effects in writing.

- I can add well chosen detail to interest the reader.

- I can summarise a paragraph.

- I can organise my writing into paragraphs to show different information or events.

Grammar and punctuation

Sentence structure

- I can use relative clauses.

- I can use adverbs or modal verbs to indicate a degree of possibility.

Text structure

- I can build cohesion between paragraphs.

- I can use adverbials to link paragraphs.

Punctuation

- I can use brackets, dashes and commas to indicate parenthesis.

- I can use commas to clarify meaning or avoid ambiguity.

Key Assessment Criteria: *Being a writer*

A year 6 writer

Transcription

Spelling

- I can convert verbs into nouns by adding a suffix.

- I can distinguish between homophones and other words which are often confused.

- I can spell the commonly mis-spelt words from the Y5/6 word list.

- I understand that the spelling of some words need to be learnt specifically.

- I can use any dictionary or thesaurus.

- I use a range of spelling strategies.

Handwriting

- I can choose the style of handwriting to use when given a choice.

- I can choose the handwriting that is best suited for a specific task.

Composition

- I can identify the audience for and purpose of the writing.

- I can choose the appropriate form and register for the audience and purpose of the writing.

- I use grammatical structures and features and choose vocabulary appropriate to the audience, purpose and degree of formality to make meaning clear and create effect.

- I use a range of sentence starters to create specific effects.

- I can use developed noun phrases to add detail to sentences.

- I use the passive voice to present information with a different emphasis.

- I use commas to mark phrases and clauses.

- I can sustain and develop ideas logically in narrative and non-narrative writing.

- I can use character, dialogue and action to advance events in narrative writing.

- I can summarise a text, conveying key information in writing.

Grammar and punctuation

Sentence structure

- I can use the passive voice.

- I vary sentence structure depending whether formal or informal.

Text structure

- I can use a variety of organisational and presentational devices correct to the text type.

- I write in paragraphs which can clearly signal a change in subject, time, place or event.

Punctuation

- I can use the semi-colon, colon and dash.

- I can use the colon to introduce a list and semi-colon within lists.

- I can use a hyphen to avoid ambiguity.

Assessment Template

This section provides a simple template that school leaders can use to record the outcomes of their assessment.

Assessment and tracking

Basic level

It is important that you have secure knowledge of how well pupils are attaining in relation to expectations. As the National Curriculum only defines end of key stage expectations for history, you need to be clear about your milestones for each year group. A possible suggestion for this is included earlier in this publication.

Essentially, you need to know whether pupils are:

- Below the expectation
- Meeting the expectation
- Exceeding the expectation

The chart on the next page would help you record this. It is suggested that you have one chart like this for each cohort in your school (i.e. it follows the cohort as they progress). This means that you can compare their year-on-year progress; noting you will need to take account of changes to the cohort.

Digging deeper

In order to take your tracking and evaluation to a deeper level, it would be helpful to consider pupils groups within your school, e.g. gender, ethnicity, pupil premium, vulnerable groups etc. You need to be exploring whether there are differences in the achievement of different groups.

Cohort tracker for English

	Year 1	Year 2	Year 3	Year 4	Year 5	Year 6
Below expectations						
Meeting expectations						
Exceeding expectations						

Achievement in English

	Strengths	Next steps
Standards by the end of KS1		
Standards by the end of KS2		
Achievement judgement		
Use of English skills in all other curriculum areas		
Use of computing skills in English		

Achievement in English

	Strengths	Next steps
How well are gaps being narrowed between vulnerable groups?		
Other issues		

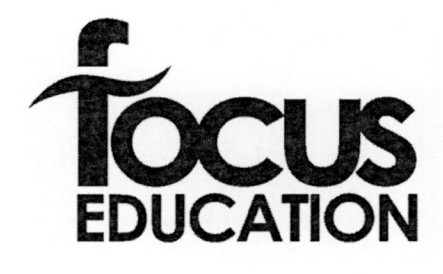

Evaluating English

This section enables school leaders to evaluate their English curriculum and arrive at an overall judgment for the quality of their setting's curriculum.

Evaluating English in your school

There are criteria for the areas identified in the diagram below.

It is important that the criteria are not used a checklist.
They must be applied adopting a 'best fit' approach.

Note that if any element is inadequate, it is likely that the overall judgement will be inadequate.

Leaders may find it helpful to highlight text.

This evaluation can then be used to identify next steps for improvement.

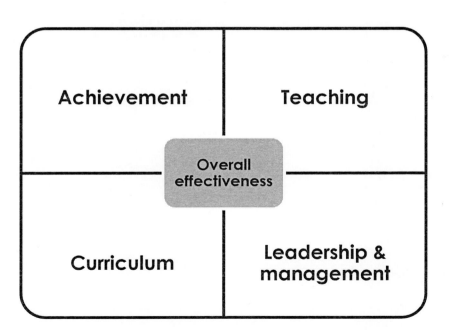

Achievement of pupils in English

Outstanding	<ul><li>Pupils show high levels of achievement in the different areas of English (reading, writing, speaking and listening) and exhibit very positive attitudes towards the subject.</li><li>Pupils rapidly acquire secure knowledge of letters and sounds and make sustained progress in learning to read and to write legibly and fluently.</li><li>Pupils express their ideas fluently and imaginatively in both writing and speaking. They are very keen readers and show a mature understanding of a wide range of challenging texts, both traditional and contemporary.</li><li>Pupils' writing shows a high degree of technical accuracy. Pupils write effectively across a range of genres, frequently showing creativity in their ideas and choice of language.</li><li>Pupils have a mature understanding of the differences between written and spoken language. They speak confidently and with maturity in relation to their age, using Standard English very effectively when required.</li><li>Pupils have learnt to be effective independent learners, able to think for themselves and to provide leadership in learning, while also being sensitive to the needs of others.</li></ul>
Good	<ul><li>Pupils acquire secure knowledge of letters and sounds and make good progress in learning to read and to write legibly and fluently.</li><li>Pupils perform equally well in reading, writing, speaking and listening. They enjoy English lessons and express their ideas confidently and with some originality in both writing and speaking.</li><li>Pupils enjoy reading a wide range of texts and can talk and write with understanding about them. They enjoy writing and write confidently for different purposes and audiences, showing a good degree of technical accuracy.</li><li>Pupils are able to vary their language according to the particular demands of the task, both spoken and written, making effective use of Standard English when required.</li><li>Pupils express their ideas clearly and well in discussion and work effectively in different groups. They are able to show independence and initiative, for instance raising thoughtful questions or helping to drive forward group work.</li></ul>
Requires Improvement	<ul><li>There is noticeable variability in pupils' performance across reading, writing, speaking and listening.</li><li>Pupils' progress in acquiring a secure knowledge of letters and sounds, or in learning to read and to write legibly and fluently, is inconsistent.</li><li>Pupils are willing to contribute and listen to discussion. Oral contributions tend to be brief or lack depth.</li><li>Pupils usually enjoy the reading introduced by the teacher. They struggle to understand more complex texts and rarely choose to extend their reading independently.</li><li>Pupils sometimes write at length but their range of language forms and vocabulary is limited. Their accuracy in spelling, grammar or punctuation lacks consistency and the quality of presentation may be variable. Pupils are not always able to observe the features of Standard English in their speech or writing when appropriate.</li></ul>
Inadequate	<ul><li>.Pupils have significant weaknesses in key areas of reading, writing, speaking or listening which limit their achievement overall. They are too often passive in lessons and show no real enthusiasm for English.</li><li>Pupils make insufficient progress in acquiring a secure knowledge of letters and sounds or in learning to read and to write legibly and fluently.</li><li>Pupils do not read for pleasure and show limited understanding when talking about their reading. They lack confidence in writing and struggle to write independently. Their writing tends to be short and contains too many inaccuracies in spelling, grammar or punctuation, with little originality.</li><li>Pupils do not express their ideas well in discussion. They tend to speak and write colloquially and are not able to use Standard English appropriately.</li><li>Pupils rarely use initiative and are highly reliant on their teacher for ideas and guidance.</li></ul>

Achievement of pupils in English (self-evaluation)

Best fit judgment	
Evidence for this judgment	
Next steps	

Quality of teaching in English

Outstanding	• Pupils' language needs and their interests in literature and other media are addressed through the imaginative use of a wide range of resources, including ICT and moving image texts. • Pupils are fully engaged through innovative classroom approaches, including well-planned drama activities. • The teaching of phonic knowledge, skill and understanding is systematic, highly enjoyable and quickly enables pupils to read fluently and write with confidence and accuracy. • Pupils make real progress in their own work as a consequence of teachers demonstrating high standards in their own use of English. Progress is aided through teachers' powerful modelling of the processes of reading and writing. Pupils are made aware of the importance of English to the world beyond school. • Teachers' expert knowledge of texts is used successfully to extend and deepen pupils' understanding. Pupils' personal responses to, and their thinking about, literature and other texts are prompted by questioning which frequently probes pupils' understanding of language. • Teachers' very good understanding of the English language ensures that the technical features of language are very well taught, including the differences between talk and writing. Systematic approaches to target-setting, marking, feedback and peer- and self-assessment, support and challenge all pupils to make precise improvements to their written or oral work.
Good	• Pupils' engagement in English, leading to good progress in reading, writing, speaking and listening, is achieved through effective use of a wide range of good-quality literary, media and other resources. Pupils learn to appreciate the importance of English in the wider world. • Pupils read fluently and write with confidence and accuracy because the teaching of phonic knowledge, skill and understanding is systematic and enjoyable. • Teachers' use of English in the classroom is well considered and effective, helping pupils to develop a good insight into how writers and others create effects. Questioning successfully engages pupils in extending their understanding of language and draws out their personal response to aspects of literature and other texts. • Pupils' wider, independent reading is stimulated because teachers share their understanding of a wide range of classic and contemporary texts with pupils. Activities are varied and imaginative, engaging pupils well through drama and varied discussion work. • Teachers understand how language works and use this knowledge effectively to develop learning. ICT, including moving image work, is well-integrated in lessons and contributes positively to pupils' progress in English. • Feedback from target-setting, marking and peer- and self-assessment is constructive and clearly identifies the next steps in pupils' written or oral work.
Requires Improvement	• Although most pupils are involved through the effective use of a wide range of resources and active approaches, including small group and pair work, teaching does not succeed in motivating or engaging all pupils equally well. • Not all pupils make good progress, although the teaching of phonic knowledge, skill and understanding has been planned carefully. There are inconsistencies in practice and in pupils' progress, although teaching promotes skill and fluency in reading and handwriting. • Most lessons are well-planned and lively and sometimes include opportunities for drama and moving image work. On occasion, the learning focus is not sufficiently sharp and the range of needs may not be fully met. ICT is used from time to time to develop independent learning and improve the quality of presentation. • Competent subject knowledge ensures that pupils read and write about a wide range of texts with competent understanding, and teachers encourage pupils. Teachers mostly use English well. Questioning extends pupils' understanding of language and literature and other texts, though it is not always sufficiently probing. • Regular and clear feedback helps pupils to understand strengths and weaknesses in their written and oral work, though it may lack precision or consistency.
Inadequate	• Significant numbers of pupils are sometimes bored, passive or badly behaved as a result of teaching failing to engage pupils. • The teaching of phonic knowledge, skill and understanding is insufficiently well- planned or delivered. • Teachers' subject knowledge is limited in key aspects of reading, writing, and speaking and listening. There are occasional weaknesses in the teacher's own understanding and use of language. • There is an imbalance of work across reading, writing, speaking and listening. Adequate learning is not secured as the resources and strategies used are limited. Pupils are not helped to appreciate the importance of English in their lives outside school.

Best fit judgment	
Evidence for this judgment	
Next steps	

Quality of the curriculum in English

Outstanding	• The curriculum is distinctive, innovative and planned very well to meet the needs of all pupils in reading, writing, speaking and listening. • Imaginative approaches, experience of a wide range of challenging texts, and clear focus on basic literacy skills ensure a rich curriculum accessible to all groups, that enables pupils to make very good progress across the different areas of English. • The curriculum is continually reviewed and improved in the light of national developments. Key aspects such as poetry, drama and media work are fully integrated into the curriculum and help to provide a rich and varied programme for pupils. Schemes of work build clearly towards productive outcomes for pupils, involving real audiences and purposes; this helps pupils to appreciate the importance of English to their lives outside school. • Independent learning and wide reading are very effectively promoted. The curriculum builds systematically on technological developments in communications and pupils have regular opportunities to use ICT and mixed media, including analysing and producing media texts. • Pupils' learning is very well enhanced by enrichment activities such as theatre and cinema visits, drama workshops, reading groups, and opportunities for writers to work with pupils in school.
Good	• The curriculum has some innovative features and is well-designed around the needs of pupils in the school. It is broad and engaging, with a good range of texts and appropriate attention to basic literacy skills. A variety of approach helps pupils to make good progress in reading, writing, speaking and listening. • The curriculum is reviewed regularly and reflects recent developments in the subject. Good attention is given to areas such as poetry, drama and media. Opportunities are taken to make direct connections between the classroom and the world beyond school. • Independent study and wider reading are well-integrated into schemes of work. ICT and mixed media are used well to help pupils develop learning in English and include work on analysing and producing moving image texts. • The curriculum incorporates regular opportunities to meet with practitioners working in English, such as writers and theatre groups.
Requires Improvement	• The curriculum requires improvement because it is not good. • The curriculum provides a reasonable balance of work that helps pupils to make progress in developing reading, writing, speaking and listening. Provision for key areas of English is built into schemes of work although there may be some variability and inconsistency in the quality of this work. The curriculum is reviewed in response to external changes and national guidance. • The curriculum is carefully planned to ensure that pupils read and write about a wide range of good-quality texts, including some media texts, and appreciate the importance of English in real-life contexts and beyond school. Some elements of ICT are built into English schemes of work, including study of media texts. Some opportunities are provided for pupils to work independently and to read outside school. • Pupils' experiences are enhanced by opportunities to watch films and plays and to work with writers, although the range of enrichment activities is limited and sometimes concentrated on support for examinations only.
Inadequate	• The curriculum does not meet the needs of significant numbers of pupils in the school and, as a result, too many make poor progress in key areas of reading, writing, speaking and listening. • Too many pupils are not engaged by the subject and do not understand its relevance to their own life. • The curriculum lacks breadth and balance. It is limited in scope, with too much concentration on a narrow range of skills. • The curriculum is not planned well enough and too little emphasis is placed on key areas of English such as poetry, drama and media work, as well as on the development of literacy skills, such as punctuation, grammar and spelling. • There is little by way of enrichment activity apart from a few activities that tend to be directly related to examination study.

Quality of the Curriculum in English (self-evaluation)

Best fit judgment	
Evidence for this judgment	
Next steps	

Quality of leadership in, and management of, English

Outstanding	• Subject leaders inspire pupils and colleagues through a passionate commitment to the subject and very good subject knowledge. • Subject leaders are very well- informed about developments in the subject nationally and use this to improve the curriculum and teaching. Innovation and creativity are evident. • All staff work very well together because there is a strong shared purpose and commitment to the same goals. Provision for pupils is reviewed collaboratively and good practice is routinely and effectively shared. • Subject responsibilities are well- delegated and all members of the team, including NQTs, have very good opportunities to contribute to developments. • Subject leaders make thoughtful and thorough use of a wide range of evidence, including the response of pupils, to review the impact of work across reading, writing, speaking and listening. As a result, self-evaluation is rigorous and effective, leading to well-targeted support for all staff. • Subject plans identify very clearly how teaching is to be further improved. There are excellent policies which support consistency, promote high levels of literacy and contribute to pupils' excellent progress in English. • The very good quality of its work means that the English department has a very high profile in the life of the school and is at the cutting edge of initiatives locally or nationally.
Good	• Subject leaders have identified clear aims for English within the school which are well-informed by national developments in the subject, and this helps to provide good direction to English work. • Teachers work well together and are keen to review practice and share ideas. • Subject leaders encourage teachers to be imaginative in their approaches to learning. Because of good leadership, there is a shared common purpose and a consistency of practice throughout the school in areas such as teaching and assessment and behaviour for learning. • Self-evaluation is accurate and effective, based on good analysis of pupils' skills and achievement in reading, writing, speaking and listening and well-informed evaluation of English teaching. This analysis is used well to identify teachers' training needs. • Subject plans are effective and include helpful ideas on improving the impact of teaching on learning. The well-thought-out policies support pupils' good or better progress in English. • The subject team is well- regarded within the school and contributes to developments across the curriculum, such as in literacy and improvements in teaching.
Requires Improvement	• The aims of English are clearly set out in subject documentation that is reviewed regularly and reflects developments in the subject nationally. • Subject guidance enables teachers to understand the key policies and agreed approaches in English. • Practical ideas are regularly shared between teachers and there is regular access to appropriate professional development. • Teachers are encouraged to share ideas and learn from each other. • Provision in the subject is regularly reviewed and systematic monitoring includes evidence from lesson observations, work sampling and analysis of pupils' progress in reading, writing, speaking and listening. • There is some recognition of areas of weakness in English, though subject plans may not be clear and specific in detailing what needs to be done to improve teaching or raise standards. • There is some recognition across the school that there is good practice in English but also an acknowledgement that it is not sufficiently consistent across all classes and for all groups.
Inadequate	• Weaknesses in subject leadership mean there is little sense of direction or identity for English. • The curriculum does not develop sufficiently quickly to meet pupils' changing needs. • Gaps in subject knowledge or leadership mean that there is little capacity to improve achievement in the subject. • Some teachers lack the necessary subject expertise. Communication between teachers may be limited and there are few opportunities for teachers to learn from each other and share good practice. • There is a lack of systematic monitoring and evaluation, leading to inaccurate subject self-evaluation and limited opportunities for further professional development. • There is insufficient understanding of how to raise standards or improve teaching in English.

Best fit judgment	
Evidence for this judgment	
Next steps	

The overall effectiveness of English education provided in the school	
Outstanding	<ul><li>English teaching is outstanding and, together with a rich and relevant English curriculum, contributes to outstanding learning and achievement. Exceptionally, achievement in English may be good and rapidly improving.</li><li>Pupils, and particular groups of pupils are well-equipped for the next stage in their education, training or employment as a result of excellent educational experiences.</li><li>Practice in the subject consistently reflects the highest expectations of staff and the highest aspirations for pupils, including disabled pupils and those with special educational needs, those for whom English is an additional language and those known to be eligible for the pupil premium.</li><li>Best practice is spread effectively in a drive for continuous improvement.</li></ul>
Good	<ul><li>Pupils benefit from English teaching that is at least good and some that is outstanding. This promotes very positive attitudes to learning and ensures that pupils' achievement in English is at least good.</li><li>Pupils and particular groups of pupils have highly positive educational experiences in English that ensure that they are well prepared for the next stage in their education, training or employment.</li><li>Pupils' progress is not held back by an inability to read or write accurately and fluently.</li><li>The school takes effective action to enable most pupils, including disabled pupils, those with special educational needs and those known to be eligible for the pupil premium, to reach their potential in English.</li></ul>
Requires Improvement	<ul><li>English in the school requires improvement because one or more of the key judgements for achievement; behaviour and safety (in English); the quality of teaching; the curriculum; and the quality of leadership and management of English requires improvement (grade 3).</li></ul>
Inadequate	English in the school is likely to be inadequate if inspectors judge any of the following to be inadequate:<ul><li>the achievement of pupils in English</li><li>the quality of teaching in English</li><li>the behaviour and safety of pupils in English</li><li>the quality of the curriculum in English</li><li>the quality of the leadership in, and management of, English.</li></ul>

Best fit judgment	
Evidence for this judgment	
Next steps	

Mapping Coverage

The 2014 curriculum gives little guidance as to text types and range of content. As Subject Leader, it is essential to ensure that there is adequate and secure understanding of all text types so that pupils make good progress in reading and writing.

The following pages gives a suggested overview of the teaching of text types across the school. As well as ensuring coverage, it also addresses progression. The document may act as a starting point for Subject Leaders to develop such an overview for their school.

The elements identified for each year group are the essentials to be explicitly taught and offer progression from Reception through to Year 6. They are the non-negotiables for each year group and all pupils would be expected to understand, use and apply each text type identified by the end of the year.

Text types will be revisited for real purposes across the curriculum in KS1 and 2 following the explicit teaching. For example, while the explicit teaching of instructions takes place in Year 2, there will be many opportunities within English and across the curriculum to use, apply and extend instructional writing in purposeful contexts from Year 3 onwards.

Similarly, it does not prevent pupils from working on text types not identified as a non- negotiable for their year group. For example, Year 2 and Year 3 pupils may well encounter persuasive texts before the non-negotiable teaching in Year 4, 5 and 6 and Year 1 pupils may write instructions for a specific purpose before the explicit teaching in Year 2.

	Reception	Year 1	Year 2	Year 3	Year 4	Year 5	Year 6
NARRATIVE	Write a meaningful sentence or sequence of sentences.	Narrative with beginning, middle and end based on familiar stories, drawing on some key narrative language.	Narrative based on a familiar story with one or more elements changed. For example: a different character, setting, event or ending. Key narrative language used.	Narrative with sequential structure - Opening - introduction of characters or setting Build-up - some indication of what the problem might be to create suspense Problem - actions and dialogue Resolution - directly linked with the problem Ending - link to the beginning, showing character's feelings or how he/she or the situation has changed.	Narrative with clear sequential structure, paragraphed accurately with a range of cohesive devices to introduce and/or link them together. Narratives with different settings; imaginary, historical etc.	Narrative told from different viewpoints. Use of narrative techniques: flashbacks; impact of different opening paragraphs; use of characters' dialogue and actions; re-purposing narrative as a play script.	Narrative structure and techniques adapted according to the type; suspense, traditional etc.
POSSIBLE TEXT TYPES	Traditional and fairy stories. Stories with familiar settings.	Traditional and fairy stories. Stories with familiar settings.	Stories with patterned language and clear narrative structures both familiar and from other cultures.	Quest and adventure stories. Legends. Stories with dilemmas.	Historical stories. Fantasy stories. Science fiction. Myths.	Fables, myths, legends. Play scripts. Stories told from a different point of view or with different "voices".	Horror/mystery stories. Classic stories.

	Reception	Year 1	Year 2	Year 3	Year 4	Year 5	Year 6
NON-NARRATIVE	Write a meaningful sentence or sequence of sentences.

Write a list. | **Recount** based on an experience, event or visit with simple orientation sentence and events in chronological order. | **Instructions** for a real purpose - recipe, plan, construction, game with a statement of purpose, list of materials/ingredients and steps in sequence. Final sentence which addresses reader - to advise, encourage, warn.

Non-chronological report written with an opening general statement or question to hook the reader, related material appropriately grouped and a closing statement with interesting fact or related to reader. | **Non-chronological report** written with an opening general statement or question to hook the reader, related material appropriately organised and paragraphed for clarity with topic sentence to open each paragraph, closing statement with interesting fact or related to reader. May also include organisational devices such as sub-headings and include diagrams etc. to add clarity. | **Explanation** with opening to introduce subject, sequence of logical steps in paragraphs introduced by topic sentences which link to the previous paragraph.

Persuasion - advert or leaflet which will include a series of points which lead to one point of view, a direct appeal to the reader, use of exaggerated, emotive language, opinions presented as fact, images, alliteration. | **Recount** - biography and autobiography. Mainly written in chronological order, but may include flashbacks. Use of first or third person as appropriate. May include opinions as well as facts and humorous or interesting incidents.

Non-chronological comparative report Compares and contrasts at least two subjects. Opening statement or question to hook reader, facts compared and contrasted by using generalisers(most, usually, many etc.) and conjunctions(while, whereas) and connecting adverbs (however, in addition, similarly).

Persuasion - one point of view Opening statement about issue and stance. Points organised in paragraphs with supporting evidence and explanation and linked with connecting adverbs. Closing statement reiterates point of view and appeals to the reader. | **Persuasion/Recount Journalistic writing.** Well-structured report with opening orientation with key facts written with deliberate bias. Includes direct and reported quotes and a final re-orientation sentence which brings the reader up to date with the current situation.

Discussion balanced argument Opening statement makes issue clear, arguments for and against presented in paragraphs with evidence and explanation to support opinion. Paragraphs and point of view clearly linked by cohesive devices. Use of impersonal language - passive voice. |

	Reception	Year 1	Year 2	Year 3	Year 4	Year 5	Year 6
POETRY	Oral recitation of rhymes and simple poems and songs. Play with rhyme and rhythm as part of phonics.	Poems to perform. Simple list poems.	Poems to perform. Calligrams. Poem based on simply structured example e.g. 1 noun, 2 adjectives, 3 adverbs, 4 verbs. Instructions for Growing Poetry by Tony Mitton.	Poems to perform List poems with extended lines. Similes. Shape poetry.	Poems to perform. Similes and metaphor to create pictures with words. Poem based on a model, drawing on the above. For example, The Magic Box by Kit Wright, Windrush Child by John Agard.	Poems to perform. Poem based on a model. For example, The Door by Miroslav Holub, Talking Turkeys by Benjamin Zephaniah. Narrative poems. For example, The Highwayman by Alfred Noyes. Word play. For example, turning descriptive language into Kennings.	Poems to perform. Personification. Use of imagery. Different poetic forms, including Shakespearean blank verse. Make choices about the form to create own poems.

It may also be useful to map across the following across the school:

- Range of literature to be read. For example – classics, modern classics, picture books
- Poetry to be read, explored and performed, including nursery rhymes
- Stories to be learned for retelling

The grid on the following page provides a template.

	Autumn 1	Autumn 2	Spring 1	Spring 2	Summer 1	Summer 2
Nursery						
Reception						
Year 1						
Year 2						
Year 3						
Year 4						
Year 5						
Year 6						

Mastery in English

What do we mean by mastery?

The concept of mastery has been introduced with the 2014 national curriculum. Mastery is not precisely defined in the national curriculum. In essence it appears that you master means that you can use the content 'upside down and inside out'.

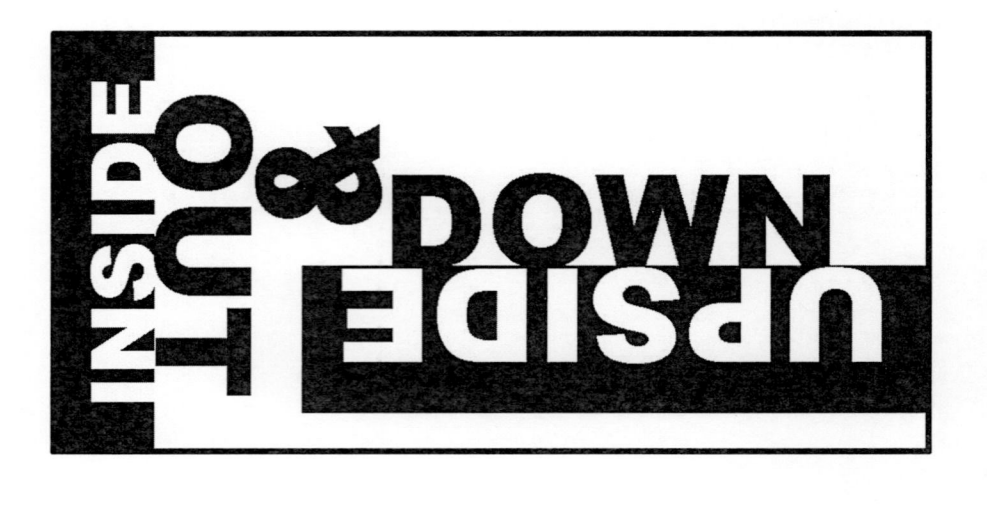

The pupils that have 'mastered' the year group expectations will be those who can use their English learning and apply it in a wide range of contexts independently without scaffolding or input. They will make independent choices about what they read with a clear purpose in mind and will structure written texts, making choices dependent on their audience and purpose.

Another way of looking at mastery

The diagram below illustrates the stages we all go through as learners on the road to 'mastering' a new concept or skill.

Consider, as an adult, your learning process in relation to this, e.g. learning to drive, cooking etc.

We are aiming to move our pupils toward being 'unconsciously competent' as learners.

Auditing Provision

The following pages offer a range of prompts and audits covering the teaching of English which may be used to establish a clear picture of the current situation and support the monitoring and evaluation process.

Reading

The Big Picture

	Red	Amber	Green
Shared expectation that every child will become the best reader possible.			
There is a positive ethos in the school which promotes and highly values reading for pleasure and for learning.			
Teachers understand how to develop children's language initially through stories, rhymes, songs and the sounds of letters; their spoken language skills and their vocabulary; the knowledge, skills and understanding needed to read and write.			
Synthetic phonics teaching is systematic and regular and characterised by pace, precision, practice and progression.			
Spoken language activities underpin writing activities which complement the development of reading.			
Interventions for younger and older struggling readers match their needs precisely and are informed by on-going assessment.			

	Red	Amber	Green
Children are grouped and taught effectively for teaching reading.			
There is an effective balance of whole-class, group, pair and individual work.			
There are early and well targeted interventions, one-to-one and small group work to enable pupils to catch up, and good links between intervention and mainstream classroom work.			
Teachers and teaching assistants , including those in KS2 are trained on how to teach reading.			
Teachers have good knowledge and understanding of the development and application of English skills in all key stages.			
There is regular formative and informative individual assessment, including assessment of phonic knowledge and skills, which is then applied to helping pupil make progress.			

Achievement

➤ What proportion of children is failing to attain age related expectations at key milestones? Is this proportion decreasing? How are you addressing this?
➤ What, if any, is the achievement gap between different groups in reading?
➤ What is the school doing to close that gap?
➤ What do you know about both standards and progress in reading in relation to different groups within your school?

Teaching

➤ How well does early teaching develop children's spoken language, familiarise them with books and extend their vocabulary?
➤ How well is reading taught?
➤ Are all staff competent teachers of reading?
➤ Is there a consistency in the way reading is taught?
➤ How well are reading skills applied across the curriculum?
➤ What is the quality of teaching for pupils who are failing to make sufficient progress?

Leadership and management

➤ To what extent does the headteacher engage him/herself in the provision for reading?
➤ To what extent are senior leaders impacting on provision for reading?
➤ What steps are leaders and managers taking to ensure absolute consistency in the teaching of reading?
➤ How well are leaders and managers using what they know from monitoring and evaluation to impact on improvement?

Behaviour and safety

➤ To what extent is any poor behaviour attributable to pupils struggling to read?

This audit may be useful as a starting point to gain an overview of the teaching of reading in the school. Information can then be used to prioritise areas which need a more specific audit in order to develop and improve.

Achievement	Red	Amber	Green
Is attainment in reading at any key stage below that found nationally?			
Is attainment below the national floor standard?			
Is attainment in reading significantly lower than other core areas?			
Is attainment of any particular group significantly lower than the average for the school and for all pupils nationally?			
Is the attainment of any broad ability group significantly lower than expected?			
Is progress significantly below year group expectations?			
Is progress for any group significantly below year group expectations?			
Is the progress for any group slower than expected?			

Strengths	Next step/s (prioritised)

Expectation and leadership	Red	Amber	Green
Are high expectations evident in classrooms?			
Are high expectations evident from leaders?			
Do you, as subject leader, have a well-evidenced overview of the strengths & weaknesses in the teaching of reading?			
Do you , as subject leader, have a clear overview of the outcomes from reading assessments and act on this to improve provision & outcomes?			
Are all staff well trained on how to actively teach reading?			
Can you evidence impact from your CPD?			

Strengths	Next step/s (prioritised)

Are there strong links between early language work in the foundation stage and work in KS1?			
Is there a shared system for tracking progress in reading across the school?			
Is there quick and effective transfer of children from one reading group to another, determined through assessment, so that teaching is matched closely to need?			
Is there a common (age appropriate) approach to the teaching of reading across the school?			
Are there strong links between intervention work and the teaching in the classroom?			
Is there a shared language for discussing reading – shared and used by children & staff?			
Is there a consistent focus on vocabulary development?			

Strengths	Next step/s (prioritised)

In lessons	Red	Amber	Green
Are key terms and vocabulary clear & explored with pupils to ensure that they recognise & understand them?			
Do teachers remind pupils of important core skills, e.g. skimming/scanning etc.?			
Do pupils have sufficient opportunities in English and in other curriculum areas to use and apply core reading skills?			
Are class novels identified for all classes and read and completed?			
Is guided reading in place and taught effectively?			
Do teachers make expectations clear before pupils begin a task?			
Do teachers give pupils frequent opportunities to discuss reading?			
Do feedback and dialogue help pupils to make progress? Is the feedback acted on by pupils?			

Strengths	Next step/s (prioritised)

Parents/Carers	Red	Amber	Green
Is there communication and training with parents/carers about how the school teaches reading?			
Do parents/carers impact positively on reading enjoyment and progress?			
Is there an effective system to link home/school reading?			

Strengths	Next step/s (prioritised)

Detailed Phonics Audit

	R/A/G	Possible Actions
Which Phonics Programme is used to systematically teach Synthetic Phonics? Is there fidelity to the programme? Have all staff involved in teaching Phonics been trained to deliver the programme? Do staff understand the programme structure and content?		
How is the teaching of Phonics organised? Grouping across whole school / Setting across a Key stage / Differentiation within cohorts / Is there evidence of differentiation for SEN /EAL learners?		
Is there a timetabled daily 20 minute Phonic session taught in school? Does planning follow a teaching sequence ?		
Is there variety in our Phonics teaching? Use of Outdoor ,active learning , games , music , good quality resources ,magnetic letters and boards , ICT		
How is the quality and effectiveness of phonics teaching monitored and evaluated? Is there a designated strategic lead for Phonics and early Reading? Are sessions observed?		
Does teachers half term / termly phonics planning reflect the length of the Phonic Phases/content of year group expectations?		
Are teachers aware of the expectations for progression through the Phonic Phases/Year Group Expectations?		
In Phonics planning are there clearly identified opportunities for children to apply their phonic knowledge and skills both indoors and outdoors ?		

	R/A/G	Possible Actions
Is there a format for tracking children through the Phonic Phases/Year group Expectations? Is the format used consistently throughout school? How often is the tracking reviewed and updated?		
Are vulnerable groups identified on tracking? Looked After Children /FSM/children with SLCN/ EAL learners / Summer Born Children		
Do all staff understand how to use the tracking sheets? Are teachers listing names of children working within a Phase and highlighting and moving children when they are secure at that Phase? Does everyone understand what we mean by 'working within' a Phase/Year Group Expectations and 'secure at' a Phase/Year Group Expectations?		
What forms of support and intervention are available to those children and groups who are not making expected progress? Pre-teaching/small group support / targeted one to one tuition / areas for support		
What arrangements are in place for transition of tracking documents? Do we moderate assessments ? What mechanisms are in place to ensure consistent assessments?		
How do we avoid repetition of the Phases/Year Group Expectations or summer learning loss? Is teacher subject knowledge secure around all Phases/Year Group Expectations in terms of coverage and expectations for children? Are effective transition procedures in place?		

	R/A/G	Possible Actions
Is Phonics data collected termly for each Year Group?		
Are teachers making effective use of the discrete teaching sequence to formatively assess children's knowledge and skills? Do Teaching Assistants make observations and record key moments in learning? Are there opportunities to discuss, record and share what is learned about children's phonic knowledge, skills and understanding during / following discrete teaching e.g. annotation of phonics planning		
Are more detailed assessments made for some individuals? How are these assessments used to target intervention or alternative provision?		
Do teachers provide child led and adult initiated opportunities to assess children's ability to blend to read in continuous provision? Are there also adult led reading activities available both indoors and outdoors? Are assessment opportunities identified in planning for phonics? Are purposeful and motivating activities planned that allow assessment of secure learning?		
Are teachers using Guided Reading Sessions to assess children's ability to blend to read? Are suitable phonically regular texts at the correct pitch being used to allow children to apply blending skills? Can children read the common exception words?		
Are teachers using evidence from independent writing ?		

Prompts for Analysis of Phonic Phase Data

- Are the vast majority of children in YR, Y1 and Y2 on track to attain age appropriate results?
  - End of YR: Secure at Phase 3/4
  - End of Y1: Secure at Phase 5/ Year Group Expectations met
  - End of Y2: Working within Phase 6+/Year Group Expectations met
- Where progress is not being made what is the reason?
- Is there a Phase or element of Year Group Expectations where progress has stalled? Why is this ? (Refer to prompts in planning tracking and assessment e.g. teacher subject knowledge and confidence in teaching and assessing certain Phases)
- Does the cohort contain a significant number of children in vulnerable groups?
- What do you notice about the groups and individuals not making expected progress?
- What will we do to accelerate progress for these children?
- Is Synthetic Phonics the right route to reading and writing for these children? Do we need to consider another path? For example Phonics by analogy, Whole Language approaches, Reading Recovery?
- Compare Phonic data from previous year – are you on track to improve outcomes? If not what is the reason?
- Compare progress of specific groups of children, e.g. Summer Born Children, FSM, Looked After Children. What do you notice?
- Identify key issues and consider how these will be addressed. Do we have staff who are knowledgeable and trained to support intervention and alternative approaches to reading and writing?
- Compare progress across the phases from autumn, to spring to summer. Identify cohorts and individuals making particularly good progress and those cohorts and children not making expected progress. How will their needs be addressed? What has worked well?
- What mechanisms are there for sharing information to ensure continuity?
- What systems are in place to transfer data ? How is this data used?

KS2 Spelling and Phonics Audit

KS2 Phonics and Spelling Audit

What is the percentage of children working below Year 2 expectations as they enter this year group?		

Planning and teaching:	**R/A/G**	**Possible Actions**
Does planning show: o that spelling is being discretely taught? o that it matches the needs of the children but has sufficiently high enough expectation? o clear routines for the teaching and learning of spelling rules and conventions? o that children are being taught spelling at age related expectation? o how additional adults support with the teaching of spelling work? Who plans and monitors this? How?		
Resources:		
Does the learning environment support children in their spelling?		
Are appropriate and useful spelling resources used?		
Application:		
Do children independently access spelling resources to support them in being independent spellers?		
Do book scrutinies evidence that children are paying attention and care to spelling?		
Can spelling work identified in planning be evidenced in children's books either as discrete teaching sessions or through the application of the content taught?		
Are children using and applying phonic/spelling knowledge across all writing opportunities?		
How are children supported/expected to use and apply spelling knowledge and strategies?		

Assessment:	R/A/G	Possible Actions
What assessments are undertaken to consider progress and next steps? How do these outcomes inform future teaching of spelling?		
Do children still working on securing phonics to Year 2 expectations have opportunities to read appropriately matched texts?		
Has the teacher secure subject knowledge to effectively teach phonics and spelling?		
How are parents/carers informed as to the routines of learning spelling?		

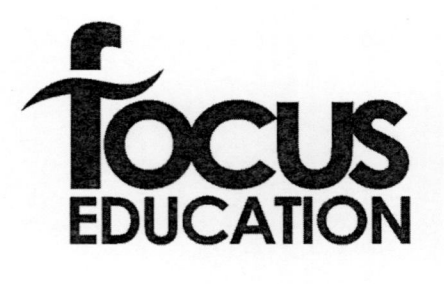

Detailed Guided Reading Audit

	R/A/G	Possible action
Is guided reading timetabled in all classes?		
Does guided reading take place in all classes?		
Are there sufficient sets of appropriate texts which offer a range of reading opportunities including poetry?		
Do teachers understand the year group expectations?		
Do teachers and other adults have good knowledge of the texts they are using?		
Do teachers plan sequences based on the year group expectations?		
Are teacher-led sessions focused on quality discussion?		
Are follow-up and independent activities learning and reading focused?		
Do pupils pre-read in preparation for their teacher-led session?		

	R/A/G	Possible action
Are strategies in place to access the guided reading text for all pupils?		
Is one guided reading session independent reading for pleasure?		
Do well - planned activities and effective organisation mean that pupils can work independently?		
Do well – planned activities based on year group learning show evidence of progress in books?		
Do all adults have the knowledge and skills to deliver guided reading?		
Are planning formats fit for purpose?		
Is there a simple process in place for recording outcomes from adult-led sessions?		
Do books and records have a body of evidence to support assessment against year group expectations?		

Reading Summary

When children enter the school...	By the end of the Foundation Stage...	By the end of Key Stage One...	By the end of Key Stage Two...

Main strengths in reading	Next steps

	Judgment by the end of... (Red/Amber/Green)				Notes	Next steps/ Actions
	Reception	Year 2	Year 4	Year 6		
Boys						
Girls						
LAC						
SEN Support						
Statement						
FSM						
EAL						
Ethnicity						

Writing

Overall Writing Audit

This audit may be useful as a starting point to gain an overview of the teaching of reading in the school. Information can then be used to prioritise areas which need a more specific audit in order to develop and improve.

Achievement	Red	Amber	Green
Is attainment in writing at any key stage below that found nationally?			
Is attainment below the national floor standard?			
Is attainment in writing significantly lower than other core areas?			
Is attainment of any particular group significantly lower than the average for the school and for all pupils nationally?			
Is the attainment of any broad ability group significantly lower than expected?			
Is progress significantly below year group expectations?			
Is progress for any group significantly below year group expectations?			
Is the progress for any group slower than expected?			

Strengths	Next step/s (prioritised)

Expectation and leadership	Red	Amber	Green
Are high expectations evident in classrooms?			
Are high expectations evident from leaders?			
Do you, as subject leader, have a well-evidenced overview of the strengths & weaknesses in the teaching of writing?			
Do you , as subject leader, have a clear overview of the outcomes from writing assessments and act on this to improve provision & outcomes?			
Are all staff well trained on how to teach writing, including grammar?			
Can you evidence impact from your CPD?			

Strengths	Next step/s (prioritised)

Consistency	Red	Amber	Green
Are there strong links between early language work in the foundation stage and work in KS1?			
Is there a shared system for tracking progress in writing across the school?			
Is the role of spoken language in the writing process understood and planned for ?			
Is there a common (age appropriate) approach to the teaching of writing across the school?			
Are there strong links between intervention work and the teaching in the classroom?			
Is there a shared language for discussing writing, including grammatical terminology – shared and used by children & staff?			
Is there a consistent focus on vocabulary development?			

Strengths	Next step/s (prioritised)

In lessons	Red	Amber	Green
Is key terminology and vocabulary clear & explored with pupils to ensure that they recognise and understand them?			
Do teachers make it clear that writing skills need to be used and applied whenever pupils are writing, not just in English lessons?			
Do pupils have sufficient opportunities in English and in other curriculum areas to use and apply core reading skills?			
Is an effective teaching sequence planned which includes responding to the context and book talk, reading as a writer, spoken language, gathering ideas, the teaching of grammar, oral rehearsal and editing and proof-reading?			
Are teachers planning with and re-visiting the year group expectations?			
Are planning formats fit for purpose?			
Are high quality texts, including poetry being used to inspire writing?			
Are pupils securing understanding of how to write a range of text types?			
Is the range of text types taught in each year group appropriate?			

	Red	Amber	Green
Is guided writing in place and taught effectively?			
Do teachers make expectations clear before pupils begin a task?			
Do teachers give pupils frequent opportunities to discuss and to evaluate their writing?			
Do teachers identify when it is important to use Standard English and for pupils to respond in complete sentences?			
Are there sufficient opportunities for oral rehearsal before writing?			
Does oral rehearsal require pupils to use Standard English in full sentences which they will need for their writing?			
Does feedback help pupils to make improvements? Is the feedback acted on by pupils?			

Strengths	Next step/s (prioritised)

Parents/Carers	Red	Amber	Green
Is there communication and training with parents/carers about how the school teaches writing?			
Do parents/carers impact positively on writing enjoyment and progress?			
Is there an effective system to link home/school writing?			

Strengths	Next step/s (prioritised)

Grammar

Is grammar taught in each year group?	R/A/G	Next Steps
Year 1		
Year 2		
Year 3		
Year 4		
Year 5		
Year 6		

How is it taught?	R/A/G	Possible Actions
Embedded in a unit of English?		
With relevant grammatical features taught and applied in context?		
With consistent use of terminology by all adults and children?		
With evident progression?		
In modelled, shared and guided writing?		
With links, consolidation and practice in guided reading? Opportunities to understand the writer's craft?		

Subject Knowledge	R/A/G	Possible Actions
Are all teachers confident?		
Are all other adults confident?		
Is Standard English used and modelled consistently, as appropriate?		
Do all teachers understand progression in the teaching and learning of grammar?		
Is there a common approach to the teaching of grammar across the school?		
Do all teachers understand the role of grammar in improving and raising standards in writing?		

Monitoring	R/A/G	Possible Actions
Is English planning monitored for the teaching of grammar?		
Do observations and drop-ins show evidence of the effective teaching and learning of grammar?		
Are books scrutinised for evidence of children learning grammatical features and applying them?		
Do children's writing targets include targets related to grammatical features?		
Is CPD for all adults matched to areas for development in the teaching and learning of grammar? Is the impact of this evaluated?		

Writing Summary

When children enter the school...	By the end of the Foundation Stage...	By the end of Key Stage One...	By the end of Key Stage Two...

Main strengths in writing	Next steps

	Judgment by the end of... (Red/Amber/Green)				Notes	Next steps/ Actions
	Reception	Year 2	Year 4	Year 6		
Boys						
Girls						
LAC						
SEN Support						
Statement						
FSM						
EAL						
Ethnicity						

Detailed intervention Audit

Which reading/writing interventions are currently being used for pupils in FS and KS1?	
Which reading/writing interventions are currently being used for pupils in KS2?	

	R/A/G	Possible actions
Are pupils identified effectively for involvement in intervention?		
Is intervention early/rapid enough?		
Is pre-teaching used as an intervention?		
Do all adults delivering interventions have the appropriate knowledge and skills?		
Are pupils who are targeted for intervention tracked?		
Are class teachers reinforcing the focus of the intervention in the classroom?		
Is the impact of the intervention evaluated?		
Are these pupils tracked following intervention?		

The Learning Environment

Learning Environment	R/A/G	Possible Actions
Is there a range of reading material available? • Poetry, including anthologies • Plays • Chapter books/novels • Classics – modern and traditional • Information books • Books representing a range of cultures • Puzzle books • Comics, magazines & newspapers • Children's own published texts • Audio texts • Dual language texts • ICT based texts		
Is the library accessible and attractive?		
Are books well ordered, accessible and well labelled?		
Are classroom book areas attractive and inviting?		
Are class libraries well ordered, accessible and well labelled?		
Is there an element of interactivity in class book areas?		
Is reading featured on displays around the school?		
Do displays evidence reading which has taken/is taking place?		
Do displays encourage reading?		

	R/A/G	Possible Actions
Do you know what children think about reading?		
Do you know what parents/carers think about reading?		
Do you have a range of reading-related events throughout the year?		
When you walk around the school, does it feel like a place where reading matters?		
Do staff model themselves as readers?		
Do extra curricular clubs include reading?		
Are parents supporting their child as a reader?		
Are parents supported with the types of text to choose for their child?		
Do you have a reading buddy system in place to promote older children taking responsibility for younger children?		

Learning Environment	R/A/G	Possible Actions
Are there working walls in classrooms which are explicit visual representations of the sequence for writing?		
Are there useful prompts related to current learning?		
Are prompts visible and accessible? For example, not too high or too many.		
Is there an appropriate range of dictionaries and thesauruses available?		
Is there a range of writing materials and implements?		
Is writing displayed around the school?		
Do displays encourage writing?		

Do you know what children think about writing?		
Do you know what parents/carers think about writing?		
Do you have a range of writing-related events throughout the year?		
When you walk around the school, does it feel like a place where writing is valued?		
Do staff model themselves as writers?		
Do extra curricular clubs include writing?		
Are parents supporting their child as a writer?		
Are parents supported with how to encourage their children to write?		

Monitoring and evaluation

Monitoring and evaluation

Subject leader monitoring is crucial if you are to make judgments about the quality and success of a subject. It is one of the most difficult things to arrange given the time constraints and fact that there are many subjects to monitor.

Senior leaders will need to make decisions about how and when to monitor subjects. This may involve a rolling programme or build on a system of focused and surface monitoring. Your Monitoring and Evaluation Policy will outline clearly which subjects are to be monitored when and by whom.

Monitoring need not be time consuming provided time is well planned and those undertaking the monitoring are prepared to make judgments without too much deliberation.

Critically, before starting, make sure you know:

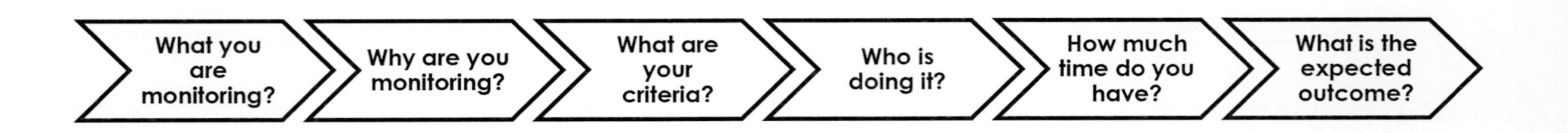

Are you clear about the difference between monitoring and evaluating?

Whilst this sounds obvious, many people slip into the trap of monitoring without due regard for evaluation. This often means that the monitoring is a complete waste of time as it does not impact on any changes being made.

Monitoring

- Gathering evidence
- Checking

Evaluating

- Asking, 'So what...?'
- What does this mean for next steps?
- What's working well? What needs improving?

You need some kind of monitoring and evaluation in order to assess the **IMPACT** of your actions.

Types of monitoring

There are many ways you can monitor. There is no one right or wrong way. It is important for subject leaders to use their time wisely in order to get the best overview possible. This often means that lesson observations are not a productive way of monitoring due to the time taken.

It is important not to under estimate the usefulness of other types of monitoring which can give you an instant whole school or key stage snap shot. These are some of the ways that subject leaders can find out about what is going on:

Lesson observations	Work sampling/scrutiny
Moderation	Scrutiny of planning
Scrutiny of assessments	Analysing data
Pupil discussion	Discussion with staff
Discussion with parents/carers	Learning Environment/Displays
Questionnaires	Pupil shadowing

Monitoring overload

It is obviously important that any monitoring is planned and known about by all staff. This planning is critical in order to ensure that staff do not feel over-burdened with monitoring. If well planned, there is no reason for anyone to feel anxious about subject leader monitoring as it should be helpful in securing a better deal for the children. Some schools have found it useful to use an evidence trail or focused evaluation approach to focus their monitoring and evaluation. This is tried and tested as an effective way of working with subject leaders. When well used it will:

➢ provide clarity of focus;
➢ structure what needs to be done; and
➢ provide a clear framework for recording findings and actions.

The following pages outline a simple overview of this approach.

It is important that agreed actions identify people and timescales in order to hold others to account; i.e. ensuring that all actions are not the sole responsibility of the subject leader.

Steps in using a focused evaluation

1
- Decide the **focus** of the evidence trail.
- Express this as a question.

2
- Be clear **who** is working on the evidence trail and the **time** you have available. This time should include time for monitoring and evaluation.

3
- Decide what **evidence** you are going to gather, i.e. what are you looking at. Be specific: e.g. if you are looking at samples of work, what are you focusing on?

4
- **Do it**.
- Gather the evidence.

MONITORING

5
- **Be evaluative**.
- Ask, 'So what...?'

EVALUATION

6
- Decide **next steps**.
- This could include feedback to specific individuals or groups.

ACTION

The templates on the next two pages outline a simple format for recording focused evaluations.

Focused Evaluation

Subject	
Date	
Evaluators	
What is your focus?	
Key question/s?	

What evidence have you gathered?	What does it tell you?
Observation & teaching	
Work scrutiny	
Pupil discussion	
Assessment evidence	
Planning	
Other	

Focused Evaluation

Evaluation and outcomes What have we found?	
Action points What do we need to do next?	
Checking Has it made a difference? How do we know? Any follow up?	

Pupil questions

The questions below may be useful when talking to pupils about their English learning. They may also be used more specifically relating to reading, writing or speaking.

Pupil interview Qs

- What comes into your head when you think of English?
- Do you enjoy English?
- Which parts of English do you enjoy most/least? Why?
- Is it a useful subject? Why?
- Do you work on your own or with a partner? Which do you prefer? Why?

Targets

- How do you know how well you are doing in English?
- Do you have a English target?
- What do you have to do to achieve it?
- What have you been doing at school/home to work on your target?
- Why do you have a target?
- What was your target last term? Did you achieve it?
- What can you do now that you couldn't do before?

Looking at work

- What did you learn in English today/yesterday?
- Find a piece of work you are pleased with? Tell me about it. What did you learn that day? How might you use this in the future?
- Do you know how to improve your work?
- Do you have a chance to improve your work?
- Does the marking and feedback help you?
- Do you ever check your work to look for mistakes? Can you show me?

Triangulating your evidence

Triangulating your evidence

When making judgements about the subject area that you lead, it is important that you gather information from a range of sources in order to reach a 'best fit' evaluation.

This is often called, 'triangulating your evidence'. In other words, taking evidence from a range of sources and checking that it presents a consistent picture. If it doesn't, you need to find out why not.

The diagram opposite identifies the types of evidence you may use, e.g.

- Teaching evidence: observations, drop ins, teacher feedback, evidence from planning, evidence from pupil work.
- Data evidence: assessment data
- Pupil evidence: conversations with pupils

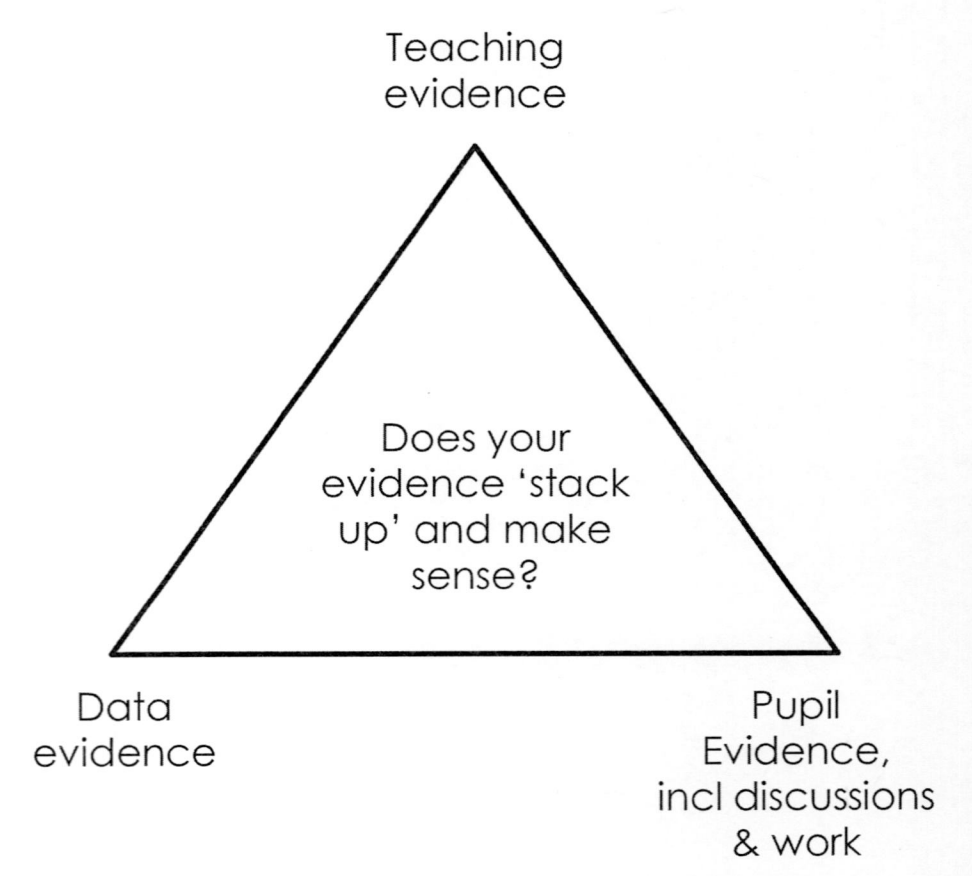

Teaching evidence

Does your evidence 'stack up' and make sense?

Data evidence

Pupil Evidence, incl discussions & work

Self-Evaluation

Self evaluation

It is good practice for subject leaders to have a simple self-evaluation record in place. This helps subject leaders identify what is going well and what needs to be improved in the subject that they are responsible for leading.

This does not need to be an overly complicated document and should be short.

Many schools present these to governors.

The self-evaluation record and action plan should fit together.

The templates on the following pages may be useful as a starting point.

Self-Evaluation Template

This section provides a simple template that school leaders can use to record the outcomes of their self evaluation.

Self-Evaluation Statement

Subject	
Date	
Subject leader	

Strength and successes How do you know?	

	Evaluation	Evidence base	Next steps...
Achievement evaluation			
Teaching evaluation			
Curriculum evaluation			
Leadership evaluation			

Self-Evaluation Statement

Financial summary	
What resources are required?	

Subject leader summary

Subject	
Date	
Subject leader	

Past	Present	Future
What have we already achieved and improved?	Where are we now? What are the headlines from our self-evaluation?	Where are we heading? What are the key action points from the curriculum action plan?

Termly Subject Leader Update

Subject	Subject leader	Academic year	Term

	Areas of strength	Areas for development	Next steps
Planning			
Work sampling			
Lesson observation & drop ins			
Pupil interviews			
Curriculum coverage			
Assessment			
Other			

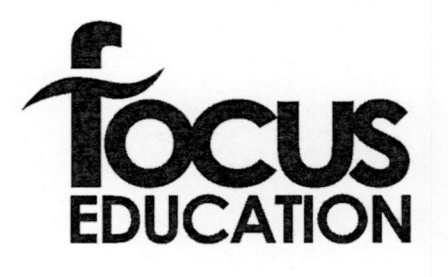

Action Planning

This section provides a simple template that school leaders can use to aid action planning.

Subject	Subject leader	Academic year

Objective (From self-evaluation)	Success criteria	Actions (who)	Time-scale	Resources/ training	Cost	Monitoring Note when actioned and how

Evaluation
(What has been the impact on outcomes and teaching?)

Additional templates

➢ Templates for recording outcomes from work scrutiny
➢ Templates for recording outcomes from pupil discussion
➢ Lesson observation record
➢ Monitoring record